SPECTRUM SERIES
PHONICS

TABLE OF CONTENTS

Grand Rapids, Michigan

INSTRUCTIONAL CONSULTANT
Mary Lou Maples, Ed.D.
Chairman of Department of Education
Huntingdon College
Montgomery, Alabama

EDITORIAL AND PRODUCTION STAFF
Series Editor: Joyce R. Rhymer; *Project Editor:* Mary Lou Griffith; *Production Editor:*
Carole R. Hill; *Senior Designer:* Patrick J. McCarthy; *Associate Designer:* Terry D. Anderson;
Project Artist: Gilda Braxton Edwards; *Artist:* Sheila Monroe-Hawkins; *Illustrators:* Carol Nicklaus, Joe Veno

Frank Schaffer Publications®

Spectrum is an imprint of Frank Schaffer Publications.

Send all inquiries to: Frank Schaffer Publications • 3195 Wilson Drive NW • Grand Rapids, MI 49534

ISBN 1-56189-941-0   8 9 10 11 12 13 VHG 09 08 07 06 05

Organized for successful learning!

The SPECTRUM PHONICS SERIES builds the right skills for reading.

The program combines four important skill strands — phonics, structural analysis, vocabulary, and dictionary skills — so your students build the skills they need to become better readers.

Four types of lesson pages offer thorough, clearly focused, systematic skills practice. That means you can focus on just the skills that need work — for the whole class, a small group, or for individualized instruction.

Short A

Name _____

Fan has the short-**a** sound. This sound is usually spelled by the letter **a**.

fan

Name the pictures. Circle each picture whose name has the short-**a** sound.

INSTRUCTION PAGE . . . The skill being covered is noted at the bottom of each student page for easy reference.

The SPECTRUM PHONICS SERIES is easy for students to use independently.

Although phonics may be an important part of a reading program, sometimes there just isn't enough time to do it all. That's why PHONICS offers uncomplicated lessons your children can succeed with on their own.

Colorful borders capture interest, highlight essential information, and help organize lesson structure. And your children get off to a good start with concise explanations and clear directions . . . followed by sample answers that show them exactly what to do.

In addition, vocabulary has been carefully controlled so your children work with familiar words. Key pictures and key words are used consistently throughout the series to represent specific sounds. And a sound-symbol chart at the back of the text helps your students quickly recall sound-symbol relationships.

Short A

Name _____

Read each sentence and the words beside it. Write the word that makes sense in each sentence.

fan

1. The van is **tan** .	tan / man / ran
2. Pam likes the blue _____.	sat / mad / hat
3. I sat on the big _____.	mat / at / am
4. The _____ is Pam's dad.	bat / man / fan
5. Jan has a red _____.	am / fan / has
6. Pat _____ in the cab.	ham / sat / bat

REINFORCEMENT PAGE . . . Comprehension exercises that use context as well as phonics skills to help build the connection from decoding to comprehension.

Turn page for more information.

Easy to manage

REVIEW PAGES . . . Frequent reviews emphasize skills application.

ASSESSMENT PAGES . . . Assessment pages give you helpful feedback on how your students are doing.

ANSWER KEY . . . Gives you the help you need when you need it — including student pages with answers for quick, easy reference.

Matching Letters

Name_____

In each row, circle the letter that is the same as the first letter in the row.

G	O	R	G	B
M	T	P	Y	M
R	N	B	R	I
B	B	O	Y	P
W	A	M	W	B
J	U	C	J	B
T	T	I	L	E

Matching Letters

Name _____

In each row, circle the letter that is the same as the first letter in the row.

a	m	(a)	h	c
d	t	o	d	r
k	w	d	t	k
f	h	t	p	f
q	q	o	g	m
c	o	z	c	g
s	w	s	m	a

6

Recognizing Letters

Name_____

All letters of the alphabet can be written in capital and small letters.
Example: **N n.** In each row, circle the letters that belong with the
first letter in the row.

S	p	(s)	t	s
f	T	O	F	F
j	J	G	O	J
O	b	o	o	m
P	p	s	t	p
I	z	i	t	i
m	A	M	N	M

Recognizing Letters

Name _____

All letters of the alphabet can be written in capital and small letters. Example: **I i.** In each row, circle the letters that belong with the first letter in the row.

c	Ⓒ	L	C	O
K	k	p	h	k
t	N	T	T	Z
Y	y	y	z	f
U	u	o	u	n
W	t	w	u	w
v	V	A	B	V

8

Beginning Sounds

Name_____

Name the pictures. In each row, circle the pictures that begin with the same sound as the first picture in the row.

Auditory discrimination of initial sounds

Name the pictures. In each row, circle the pictures that begin with the same sound as the first picture in the row.

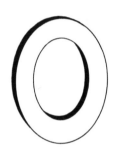			
			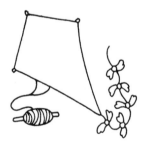
		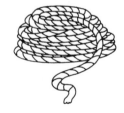	

Auditory discrimination of initial sounds

Ending Sounds

Name _____

Name the pictures. In each row, circle the pictures that end with the same sound as the first picture in the row.

Auditory discrimination of final sounds

Ending Sounds

Name the pictures. In each row, circle the pictures that end with the same sound as the first picture in the row.

Auditory discrimination of final sounds

Consonants: S

Name _____

The sound at the beginning of **sun** is spelled by the letter **s.**

sun

Name the pictures. Circle each picture whose name begins with the sound of **s.**

Auditory discrimination of initial *s*

Consonants: S

Name_____

Name the pictures. Write **s** below each picture whose name begins with the sound of **s**.

sun

_____

s

_____

_____

_____

_____

5

_____

_____

6

_____

_____

_____

_____

_____

_____

_____

_____

_____

_____

Sound-symbol association of initial *s*

Consonants: S

Name_____

Name the pictures. Draw a line from the letter **s** to the picture whose name begins with the sound of **s**.

sun

  s      s 

  s      s 

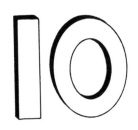  s      s 

  s      s 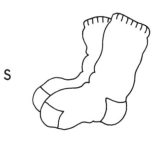

Symbol-sound association of initial *s*

Consonants: M

Name_____

The sound at the beginning of **mouse** is spelled by the letter **m.**

mouse

Name the pictures. Circle each picture whose name begins with the sound of **m.**

Auditory discrimination of initial *m*

Consonants: *M*

Name _____

Name the pictures. Write **m** below each picture whose name begins with the sound of **m.**

mouse

_____

_____

_____
- - - - - - - -
_____

_____
- - - - - - - -
_____

_____
- - - - - - - -
_____

_____
- - - - - - - -
_____

_____
- - - - - - - -
_____

_____
- - - - - - - -
_____

_____
- - - - - - - -
_____

_____
- - - - - - - -
_____

Consonants: *M*

Name _____

Name the pictures. Draw a line from each letter to the picture whose name begins with that letter.

mouse

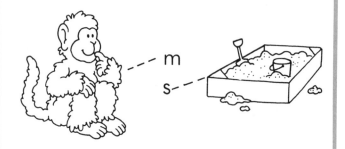
m
s

m
s

m
s

m
s

m
s

m
s
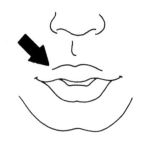

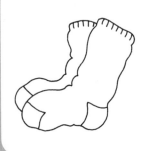
m
s

m
s

Name _____

The sound at the beginning of **tent** is spelled by the letter **t**.

tent

Name the pictures. Circle each picture whose name begins with the sound of **t**.

  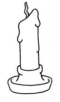

   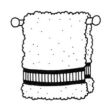

Consonants: *T*

Name_____

Name the pictures. Write **t** below each picture whose name begins with the sound of **t**.

tent

_____

t

_____

_____

_____

_____

_____

_____

_____

10

_____

Sound-symbol association of initial *t*

Consonants: T

Name the pictures. Draw a line from each letter to the picture whose name begins with that letter.

tent

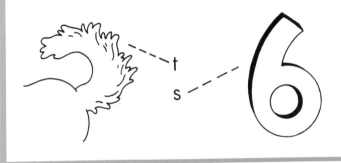 t
s

 t
m

 t
m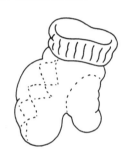

 t
s

 t
s

 t
m

 t
s

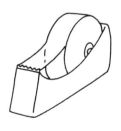 t
m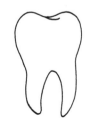

Symbol-sound association of initial *t* and other consonants

21

S, M, and T

Name _____

Name the pictures. Write the letter that stands for the beginning sound of each picture name.

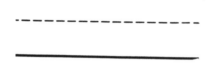
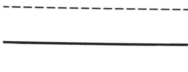

m

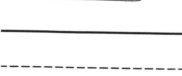

22

Ending Sounds: *S, M,* and *T*

The sound at the end of **bus** is spelled by the letter **s.**

The sound at the end of **ham** is spelled by the letter **m.**

The sound at the end of **cat** is spelled by the letter **t.**

| bu**s** |
| ha**m** |
| ca**t** |

Look at the pictures. Circle the letter that stands for the sound you hear at the end of the picture name.

s m (t)	s m t	s m t	s m t
s m t	s m t	s m t	s m t
s m t	s m t	s m t	s m t
s m t	s m t	s m t	s m t

Consonants: *P*

The sound at the beginning of **pig** is spelled by the letter **p.**

pig

Name the pictures. Circle each picture whose name begins with the sound of **p.**

 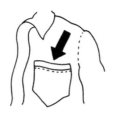  

Auditory discrimination of initial *p*

Consonants: *P*

Name_____

Name the pictures. Write **p** below each picture whose name begins with the sound of **p.**

pig

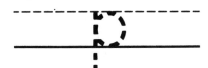
P

_____

_____

_____

_____

_____

_____

_____

_____

Sound-symbol association of initial *p*

Consonants: P

Name the pictures. Draw a line from each letter to the picture whose name begins with that letter.

pig

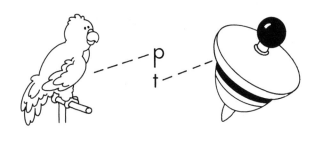
p
t

p
s

p
m

p
s

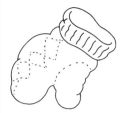
p
m

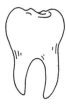
p
t

p
t
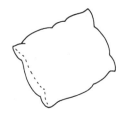

p
s

Symbol-sound association of initial *p* and other consonants

Consonants: *N*

Name _____

The sound at the beginning of **nest** is spelled by the letter **n.**

nest

Name the pictures. Circle each picture whose name begins with the sound of **n.**

   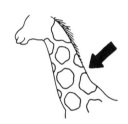

Consonants: _N_

Name the pictures. Write **n** below each picture whose name begins with the sound of **n**.

nest

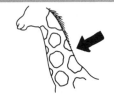

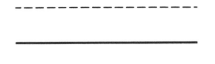

Consonants: N

Name _____

Name the pictures. Draw a line from each letter to the picture whose name begins with that letter.

nest

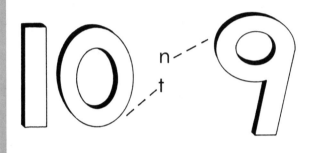

n
t

n
s

n
m

n
p

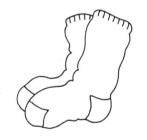

n
s

n
t

n
p

n
m

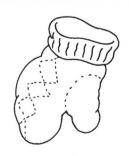

Consonants: C

Name _____

The sound at the beginning of **car** is spelled by the letter **c.**

car

Name the pictures. Circle each picture whose name begins with the sound of **c.**

Auditory discrimination of initial c

Consonants: C

Name the pictures. Write **c** below each picture whose name begins with the sound of **c**.

car

_____
_____

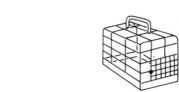

_____
_____

_____
_____

Sound-symbol association of initial c

31

Consonants: C

Name the pictures. Draw a line from each letter to the picture whose name begins with that letter.

car

 c
p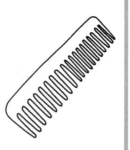

 c
n

 C
S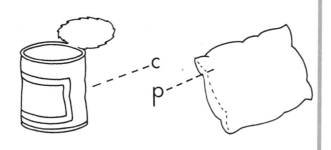

 C
t

 c
m

 c
p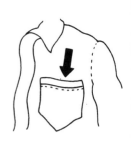

 c
m

 c
n

32

Symbol-sound association of initial *c* and other consonants

Name_____

Name the pictures. Write the letter that stands for the beginning sound of each picture name.

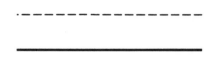
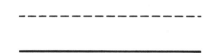

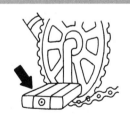

Ending Sounds: *P, N,* and *C*

Name _____

The sound at the end of **moon** is spelled by the letter **n.** The sound at the end of **mop** is spelled by the letter **p.** The sound at the end of **magic** is spelled by the letter **c.**

moo**n**
mo**p**
magi**c**

Name the pictures. Circle the letter that stands for the sound you hear at the end of each picture name.

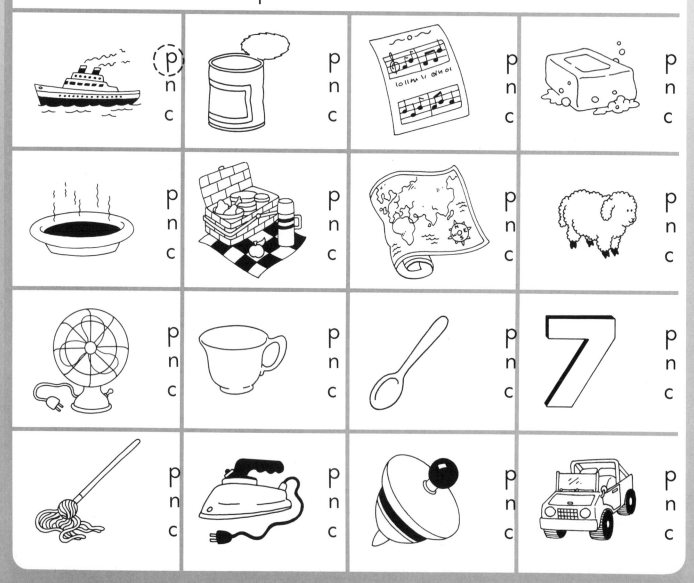

Sound-symbol association of final *p, n,* and *c*

Consonants: *K*

The sound at the beginning of **kitten** is spelled by the letter **k.**

kitten

Name the pictures. Circle each picture whose name begins with the sound of **k.**

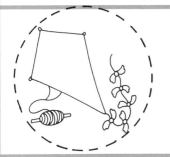   

 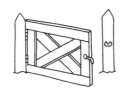  

Consonants: *K*

Name_____

Name the pictures. Write **k** below each picture whose name begins with the sound of **k**.

kitten

Sound-symbol association of initial *k*

Consonants: K

kitten

Name

Look at the pictures. Draw a line from each letter to the picture whose name begins with that letter.

k
p

k
n

k
t

k
s

k
t

k
m

k
p

k
n

Symbol-sound association of initial *k* and other consonants

37

Consonants: R

The sound at the beginning of **rose** is spelled by the letter **r.**

rose

Name the pictures. Circle each picture whose name begins with the sound of **r.**

   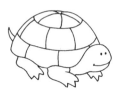

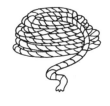   

   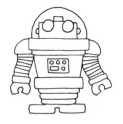

Auditory discrimination of initial r

Consonants: R

Name_____

Name the pictures. Write **r** below each picture whose name begins with the sound of **r**.

rose

_____

r̈

_____

_____

- - - - - - - - -

_____

_____

- - - - - - - - -

_____

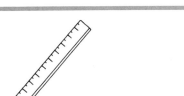

_____

- - - - - - - - -

_____

_____

- - - - - - - - -

_____

_____

- - - - - - - - -

_____

_____

- - - - - - - - -

_____

_____

- - - - - - - - -

_____

_____

- - - - - - - - -

_____

Consonants: *R*

rose

Name _____

Name the pictures. Draw a line from each letter to the picture whose name begins with that letter.

r
k

r
p

r
m

r
t

r
s

r
n

r
p

r
s

Symbol-sound association of initial *r* and other consonants

Consonants: B

Name _____

The sound at the beginning of **ball** is spelled by the letter **b.**

ball

Name the pictures. Circle each picture whose name begins with the sound of **b.**

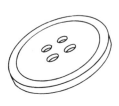

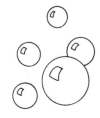

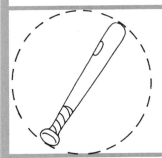

Consonants: B

Name_____

Name the pictures. Write **b** below each picture whose name begins with the sound of **b**.

ball

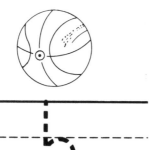

b

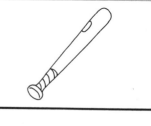

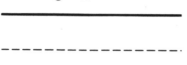

42

Consonants: *B*

Name _____

Name the pictures. Draw a line from each letter to the picture whose name begins with that letter.

ball

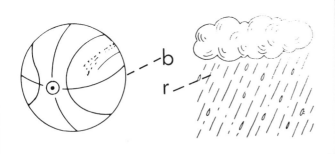
b
r

 b c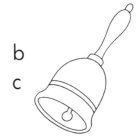

 b s

b m

 b k

b r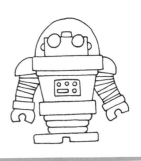

 b n

 b t

Name the pictures. Write the letter that stands for the beginning sound of each picture name.

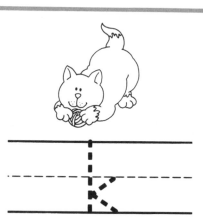

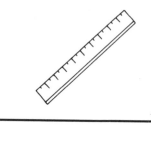

Review of sound-symbol association of initial *k*, *r*, and *b*

Ending Sounds: *K, R,* and *B*

Name _____

The sound at the end of **book** is spelled by the letter **k.** The sound at the end of **four** is spelled by the letter **r.** The sound at the end of **tub** is spelled by the letter **b.**

boo**k**
fou**r**
tu**b**

Name the pictures. Circle the letter that stands for the sound you hear at the end of each picture name.

Consonants: *J*

Name_____

The sound at the beginning of **jet** is spelled by the letter **j.**

jet

Name the pictures. Circle each picture whose name begins with the sound of **j.**

  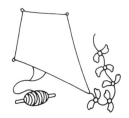 

 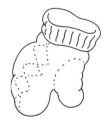  

Auditory discrimination of initial *j*

Consonants: J

jet

Name the pictures. Write **j** below each picture whose name begins with the sound of **j**.

j

Sound-symbol association of initial *j*

47

Name the pictures. Draw a line from each letter to the picture whose name begins with that letter.

jet

j
s

j
n

j
c

j
k

j
t

j
p

j
m

j
b
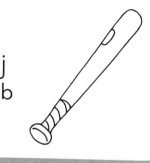

Symbol-sound association of initial *j* and other consonants

Consonants: *F*

Name _____

The sound at the beginning of **fish** is spelled by the letter **f.**

fish

Name the pictures. Circle each picture whose name begins with the sound of **f.**

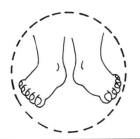   

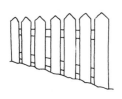   

 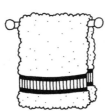  

Consonants: *F*

Name _____

Name the pictures. Write **f** below each picture whose name begins with the sound of **f.**

fish

_____
- - - - f - - - - -
_____

_____
- - - - - - - - - - -
_____

_____
- - - - - - - - - - -
_____

_____
- - - - - - - - - - -
_____

_____
- - - - - - - - - - -
_____

_____
- - - - - - - - - - -
_____

_____
- - - - - - - - - - -
_____

_____
- - - - - - - - - - -
_____

Consonants: *F*

fish

Name _____

Name the pictures. Draw a line from each letter to the picture whose name begins with that letter.

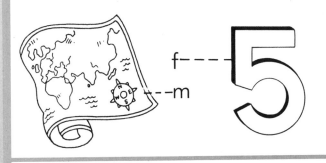

f - - - 5

- - m

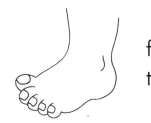 f t

 f n

 f c

 f k

 f b

 f t

 f b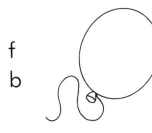

Consonants: G

Name _____

The sound at the beginning of **goat** is spelled by the letter **g.**

goat

Look at the pictures. Circle each picture whose name begins with the sound of **g.**

   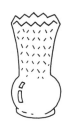      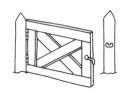

         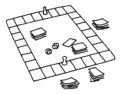

Auditory discrimination of initial *g*

Consonants: G

Name the pictures. Write **g** below each picture whose name begins with the sound of **g**.

goat

_____
g

_____

_____

_____

_____

_____

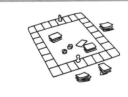

_____

_____

_____

Name _____

Look at the pictures. Draw a line from each letter to the picture whose name begins with that letter.

goat

 g
f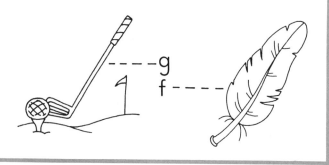

 g
p

 g
t

 g
p

 g
m

g
s

 g
b

g
r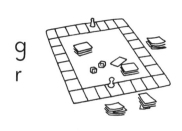

 **REVIEW** *J, F, and G*

Name _____

Name the pictures. Write the letter that stands for the beginning sound of each picture name.

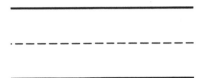

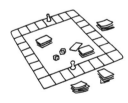

Review of sound-symbol association of initial j, f, and g

Ending Sounds: F and G

Name_____

The sound at the end of **roof** is spelled by the letter **f.** The sound at the end of **bag** is spelled by the letter **g.**

roo**f**
ba**g**

Name the pictures. Circle the letter that stands for the sound you hear at the end of each picture name.

Consonants: *H*

Name _____

The sound at the beginning of **horse** is spelled by the letter **h.**

horse

Name the pictures. Circle each picture whose name begins with the sound of **h.**

 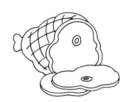  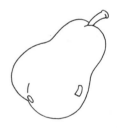

Consonants: *H*

Name _____

Name the pictures. Write **h** below each picture whose name begins with the sound of **h.**

horse

—————————
- - - **h** - -
—————————

—————————
- - - - - - -
—————————

—————————
- - - - - - -
—————————

—————————
- - - - - - -
—————————

—————————
- - - - - - -
—————————

—————————
- - - - - - -
—————————

—————————
- - - - - - -
—————————

—————————
- - - - - - -
—————————

—————————
- - - - - - -
—————————

Consonants: *H*

Name the pictures. Draw a line from each letter to the picture whose name begins with that letter.

horse

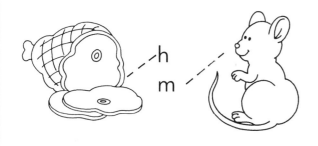
h
m

h
t

h
p

h
k

h
b

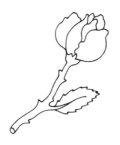
h
r
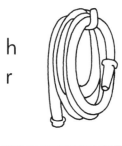

h
f

h
g

Symbol-sound association of initial *h* and other consonants

Consonants: *D*

Name _____

The sound at the beginning of **dog** is spelled by the letter **d.**

dog

Look at the pictures. Circle each picture whose name begins with the sound of **d.**

 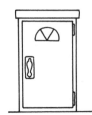  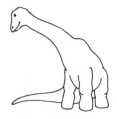

Auditory discrimination of initial *d*

Consonants: *D*

Name _____

Name the pictures. Write **d** below each picture whose name begins with the sound of **d.**

dog

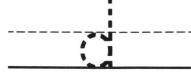

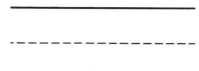

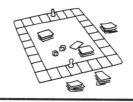

Consonants: D

Name the pictures. Draw a line from each letter to the picture whose name begins with that letter.

dog

   d   
p

   d   
c

   d   
f

   d   
t

   d
r

  d   
b

   d   
t

   d   
g

Symbol-sound association of initial *d* and other consonants

Consonants: Z

Name

The sound at the beginning of **zoo** is spelled by the letter **z.**

ZOO

Name the pictures. Circle each picture whose name begins with the sound of **z.**

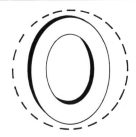 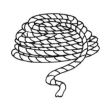  

Consonants: Z

Name _____

Name the pictures. Write **z** below each picture whose name begins with the sound of **z**.

ZOO

_____

 z _ _ _ _ _ _ _ _ _

_____

_ _ _ _ _ _ _ _ _ _ _

_____

_ _ _ _ _ _ _ _ _ _ _

_____

_ _ _ _ _ _ _ _ _ _ _

_____

_ _ _ _ _ _ _ _ _ _ _

_____

_ _ _ _ _ _ _ _ _ _ _

_____

_ _ _ _ _ _ _ _ _ _ _

_____

_ _ _ _ _ _ _ _ _ _ _

Sound-symbol association of initial z

Name _____

Name the pictures. Draw a line from each letter to the picture whose name begins with that letter.

ZOO

 z
n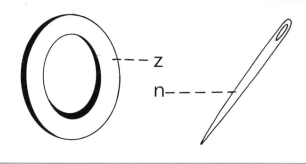

 z
p

m
s

 z
c

k
s

b
s

 r
z

 z
t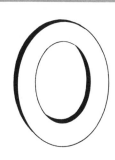

H, D, and Z

Name

Name the pictures. Write the letter that stands for the beginning sound of each picture name.

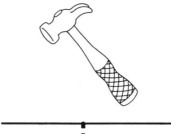      

Review of sound-symbol association of initial h, d, and z

Consonants: *W*

Name _____

The sound at the beginning of **watch** is spelled by the letter **w.**

watch

Name the pictures. Circle each picture whose name begins with the sound of **w.**

 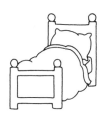  

 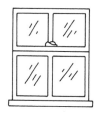 

Consonants: W

Name _____

Name the pictures. Write **w** below each picture whose name begins with the sound of **w.**

watch

_____

- - - W - - - - - - - - - - -

_____

_____

- - - - - - - - - - - - - - -

_____

_____

- - - - - - - - - - - - - - -

_____

_____

- - - - - - - - - - - - - - -

_____

_____

- - - - - - - - - - - - - - -

_____

_____

- - - - - - - - - - - - - - -

_____

_____

- - - - - - - - - - - - - - -

_____

_____

- - - - - - - - - - - - - - -

_____

_____

- - - - - - - - - - - - - - -

_____

Sound-symbol association of initial w

Consonants: W

Name the pictures. Draw a line from each letter to the picture whose name begins with that letter.

watch

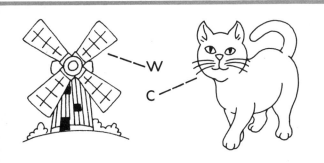
w
c

d
w

w
z

w
b

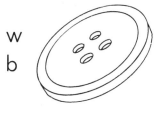

piano
w
p

window

milk
w
m

well

w
j

jar

w
g

guitar

Consonants: *V*

Name

Name _____

The sound at the beginning of **vase** is spelled by the letter **v**.

vase

Name the pictures. Circle each picture whose name begins with the sound of **v**.

   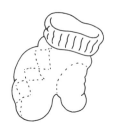

 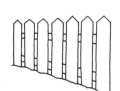  

Auditory discrimination of initial *v*

Consonants: V

Name the pictures. Write **v** below each picture whose name begins with the sound of **v**.

vase

Consonants: V

Name _____

Name the pictures. Draw a line from each letter to the picture whose name begins with that letter.

vase

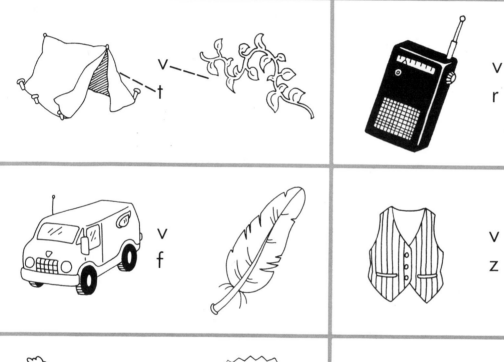

v
t

v
r

v
f

v
z

v
c

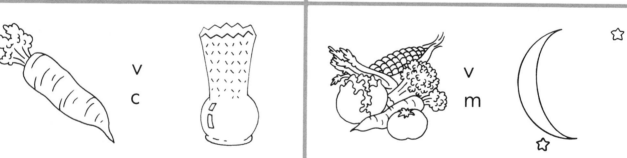

v
m

v
w

v
g

Consonants: *L*

The sound at the beginning of **lion** is spelled by the letter **l.**

lion

Name the pictures. Circle each picture whose name begins with the sound of **l.**

Auditory discrimination of initial *l*

73

Consonants: L

Name _____

Name the pictures. Write **l** below each picture whose name begins with the sound of **l**.

lion

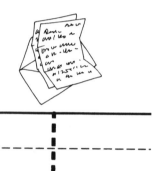

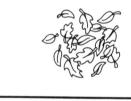

74

Sound-symbol association of initial l

Name _____

Name the pictures. Draw a line from each letter to the picture whose name begins with that letter.

l ion

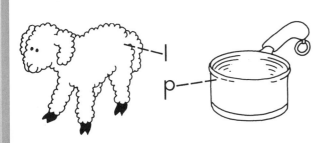

l
p

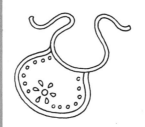

l
b

l
t

l
s

l
w

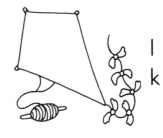

l
k

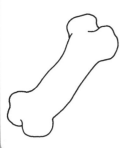
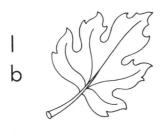

l
b

l
d

Name the pictures. Write the letter that stands for the beginning sound of each picture name.

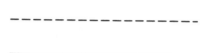

Review of sound-symbol association of initial *w, v,* and *l*

Ending Sounds: *D* and *L*

Name _____

The sound at the end of **road** is spelled by the letter **d.** The sound at the end of **girl** is spelled by the letter **l.**

roa**d**
gir**l**

Name the pictures. Circle the letter that stands for the sound you hear at the end of each picture name.

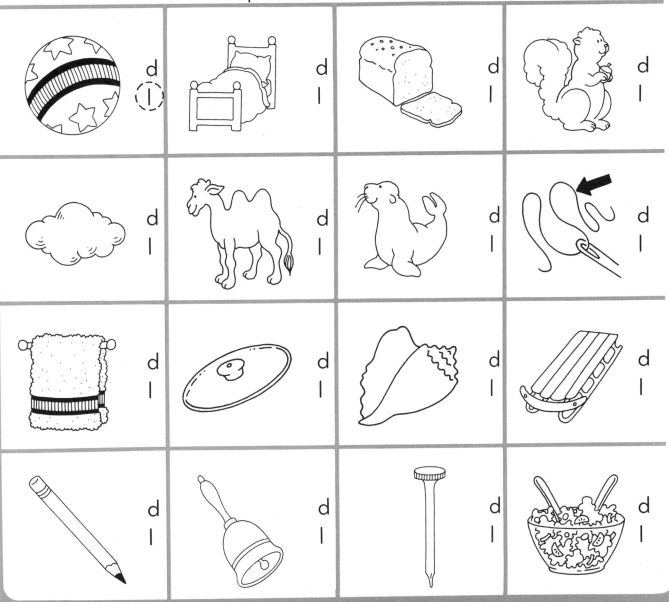

Sound-symbol association of final *d* and *l*

Consonants: *Y*

Name _____

The sound at the beginning of **yard** is spelled by the letter **y.**

yard

Look at the pictures. Circle each picture whose name begins with the sound of **y.**

Auditory discrimination of initial y

Consonants: Y

Name _____

Look at the pictures. Write **y** below each picture whose name begins with the sound of **y**.

yard

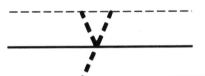

_____

___ Y ___

_____

_____

_____

_____

_____

_____

_____

_____

Consonants: Y

Name _____

Look at the pictures. Draw a line from each letter to the picture whose name begins with that letter.

yard

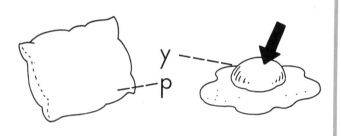

 m
n

 y
b

 y
r

 y
c

 s
t

 w
r

 y
k

Symbol-sound association of initial *y* and other consonants

The sound at the end of **ax** is spelled by the letter **x.**

a**X**

Name the pictures. Circle each picture whose name ends with the sound of **x.**

 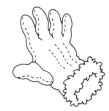 

Name _____

Name the pictures. Write **x** below each picture whose name ends with the sound of **x**.

a**x**

x

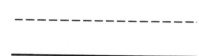

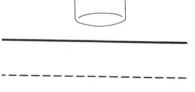

Sound-symbol association of final *x*

Consonants: X

Name _____

Name the pictures. Draw a line from each letter to the picture whose name ends with that letter.

a**x**

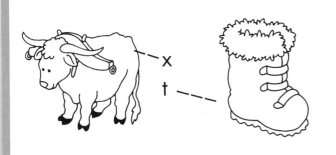
x
t

x
r

x
d

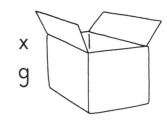
x
g

x
n

g
k

l
b

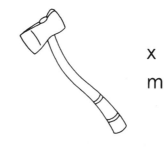
x
m

Symbol-sound association of final x and other consonants

83

Consonants: *Qu*

The sound at the beginning of **quilt** is spelled by the letters **qu.**

quilt

Look at the pictures. Circle each picture whose name begins with the sound of **qu.**

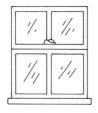  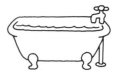

Auditory discrimination of initial *qu*

Consonants: *Qu*

Name _____

Look at the pictures. Write **qu** below each picture whose name begins with the sound of **qu.**

quilt

_____

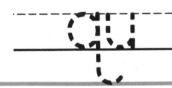

_____

_____

_____

_____

_____

_____

_____

_____

Consonants: *Qu*

Name _____

Look at the pictures. Draw a line from each letter or pair of letters to the picture whose name begins with that letter or pair of letters.

quilt

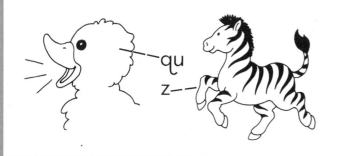

qu

z

c

g

s

k

qu

w

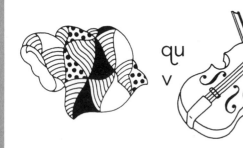

qu

v

f

j

qu

b

qu

p

Symbol-sound association of initial *qu* and other consonants

Y and Qu

Name _____

Look at the pictures. Write the letter or pair of letters that stands for the beginning sound of each picture name.

_____
qu
_____

_____
_____

_____
_____

_____
_____

_____
_____

_____
_____

_____
_____

_____
_____

_____
_____

Ending Sounds

Name _____

Name the pictures. Write the letter that stands for the ending sound of each picture name.

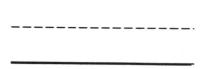

_____

m

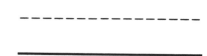

_____

_____

_____

_____

_____

_____

_____

_____

Review of sound-symbol association of final consonants

Consonants

Name _____

Name the pictures. Write the letters that stand for the beginning and ending sounds of each picture name.

d o g

u

o

o

a

u

a

i

u

Short A

Fan has the short-**a** sound. This sound is usually spelled by the letter **a.**

f**a**n

Name the pictures. Circle each picture whose name has the short-**a** sound.

90

Short A

Name the pictures. Write **a** below each picture whose name has the short-**a** sound.

f**a**n

a

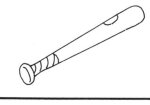

Short A

Read the words and name the pictures. Draw a line from each word to the picture it names.

fan

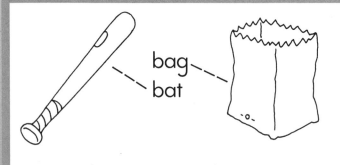

bag
bat

cap
cat

hat
ham

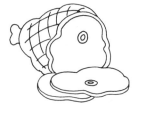

map
mat

tag
ax

van
man

pan
fan

can
cab

92

Short A

Name _____

Read each sentence and the words beside it. Write the word that makes sense in each sentence.

fan

1. The van is __tan__ .

   tan
   man
   ran

2. Pam likes the blue _____ .

   sat
   mad
   hat

3. I sat on the big _____ .

   mat
   at
   am

4. The _____ is Pam's dad.

   bat
   man
   fan

5. Jan has a red _____ .

   am
   fan
   has

6. Pat _____ in the cab.

   ham
   sat
   bat

Short *I*

Name _____

Bib has the short-i sound. This sound is usually spelled by the letter i.

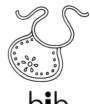

bib

Name the pictures. Circle each picture whose name has the short-i sound.

   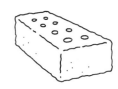

   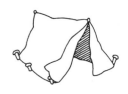

Auditory discrimination of short *i*

Short *I*

Name _____

Name the pictures. Write **i** below each picture whose name has the short-**i** sound.

b**i**b

i

_____

_____

_____

_____

_____

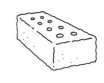

_____

_____

_____

Short *I*

Name _____

Read the words and look at the pictures. Draw a line from each word to the picture it tells about.

b**i**b

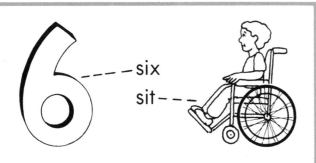

six
sit

pig
dig

mitt
mix

hit
hill

wig
win

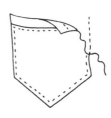

zip
rip

dig
wig

lid
lips

Short *I*

Name _____

Read each sentence and the words beside it.
Write the word that makes sense in each
sentence.

bib

1. Will this hat _____ Tim?

   fit
   wig
   did

2. Jan will _____ the car with gas.

   wig
   his
   fill

3. Jim said his cat was _____.

   ill
   is
   if

4. The pig _____ on the hill.

   six
   kid
   hid

5. Jill _____ the ball with the bat.

   hit
   his
   pin

6. Is the _____ on the pan?

   hills
   lid
   him

Short A and I

Name _____

Read the words and look at the pictures. Circle the word that tells about each picture.

pin fan fin (pan) 	hit mat mitt hat 	lid lad lap lip 
sit ax add six 	bat bit miss mad 	hit bag hat big 
cat tap cap tip 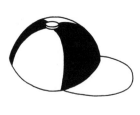	pig dam dig pass 	wag dig wig dad 
mix fat map fit 	rip sap sip ran 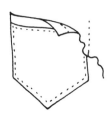	can zip cap big 

Review of symbol-sound association of short-*a* and short-*i* words

Short O

Top has the short-**o** sound. This sound is usually spelled by the letter **o.**

top

Name the pictures. Circle each picture whose name has the short-**o** sound.

  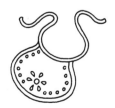 

Short O

Name _____

Name the pictures. Write **o** below each picture whose name has the short-**o** sound.

top

_____

(O)

_____

_____

_____

_____

_____

_____

_____

_____

_____

_____

_____

_____

_____

_____

_____

Sound-symbol association of short *o*

Short O

Name _____

Read the words and look at the pictures. Draw a line from each word to the picture it tells about.

top

 box fox	dots  doll dots
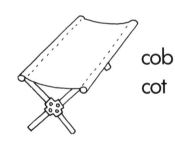 cob cot 	 hot hop 
 pop pot 	mop rod  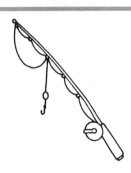
 ox top 	hog log  

Short O

Name _____

Read each sentence and the words beside it.
Write the word that makes sense in each sentence.

top

1. The doll is in the __box__.

    box
    odd
    hog

2. Todd wants help with the _____ pot.

    stop
    hot
    log

3. The _____ sat on a log.

    fox
    lot
    hot

4. Lin will get the _____ for you.

    on
    odd
    cot

5. Ron got the _____ for his dad.

    not
    mop
    on

6. Pam likes the hat with the blue _____.

    dots
    hot
    lot

Short *E*

Name _____

Bed has the short-**e** sound. This sound is usually spelled by the letter **e**.

b**e**d

Name the pictures. Circle each picture whose name has the short-**e** sound.

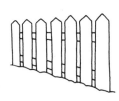  

Short *E*

Name _____

b **e** **d**

Name the pictures. Write **e** below each picture whose name has the short-**e** sound.

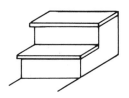

_____

_____

- - - - - - - - - - - -

_____

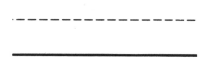

_____

_____

_____

- - - - - - - - - - - -

_____

_____

- - - - - - - - - - - -

_____

_____

- - - - - - - - - - - -

_____

_____

- - - - - - - - - - - -

_____

Sound-symbol association of short *e*

Short *E*

Name _____

Read the words and look at the pictures. Draw a line from each word to the picture it tells about.

b**e**d

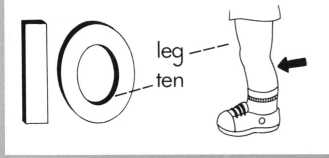

leg - - -
ten - - -

wet
jet

bell
well

pet
net

wet
web

egg
fell

men
hen

beg
bed

Short E

Name _____

Read each sentence and the words beside it. Write the word that makes sense in each sentence.

bed

1. Kim __fed__ the cat.

jet
web
fed

2. Is the _____ set to go?

met
fed
jet

3. Dad will let Len get a _____.

pet
fell
web

4. Is the pig in the _____?

beg
pen
wet

5. Ben will help fix the _____.

eggs
fell
let

6. We _____ at the play.

met
get
let

Short O and E

Name _____

Read the words and look at the pictures. Circle the word that tells about each picture.

(box)
fed
bell
fox
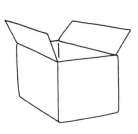

top
ten
men
mop

jet
pot
job
pet

hot
men
hen
mop

doll
pet
well
pot

egg
ox
fell
fox

wet
web
cob
cot
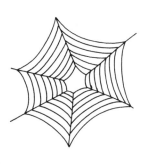

pop
ten
top
pen

tell
beg
top
bed

rod
leg
log
red

fed
hop
hen
mop

got
net
not
get

Short *U*

Name _____

Cup has the short-**u** sound. This sound is usually spelled by the letter **u.**

c**u**p

Name the pictures. Circle each picture whose name has the short-**u** sound.

 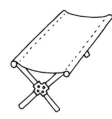  

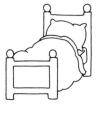   

 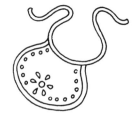  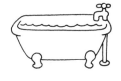

Auditory discrimination of short *u*

Short *U*

Name _____

Name the pictures. Write **u** below each picture whose name has the short-**u** sound.

cup

_____

- - - - - - **u** - - - - -

_____

- - - - - - - - - - -

_____

- - - - - - - - - - -

_____

- - - - - - - - - - -

_____

- - - - - - - - - - -

_____

- - - - - - - - - - -

_____

- - - - - - - - - - -

_____

- - - - - - - - - - -

Short *U*

Name _____

Read the words and look at the pictures. Draw a line from each word to the picture it tells about.

c**u**p

bus
sun

bun
bug

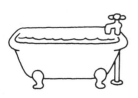
tub
hug

run
rug

cup
pup

cut
cub

mud
mug

nut
jug

Symbol-sound association of short-*u* words

Short *U*

Name _____

Read each sentence and the words beside it. Write the word that makes sense in each sentence.

cup

1. Jan put the pup into the **tub** .

cub
tub
cut

2. The cub fell into the _____ .

mud
run
nut

3. Dan put the _____ and mugs into a box.

cuts
sun
cups

4. Russ had to _____ to get help.

run
tub
mug

5. Lee will fix the _____ on his leg.

cut
jug
sun

6. Pam got the can of _____ for Mom.

cuts
nuts
mug

Short Vowels

Name

Read the words and name the pictures. Circle the word that names each picture.

(sun) suds sad sat		lid lad lip lap	

mug
mat
man
mud

cat
cob
cab
cot

bag
bed
bad
beg

pin
pen
peg
pig

ran
rug
rag
rub

bit
beg
bet
bib

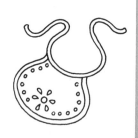

net
nut
men
met

top
tab
tub
tap

but
bat
bit
bet

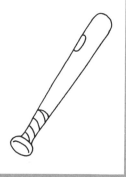

bug
but
bun
bus

Short Vowels

Name the pictures. Circle the letter that stands for the vowel sound in each picture name. Then write the letter to complete the picture name.

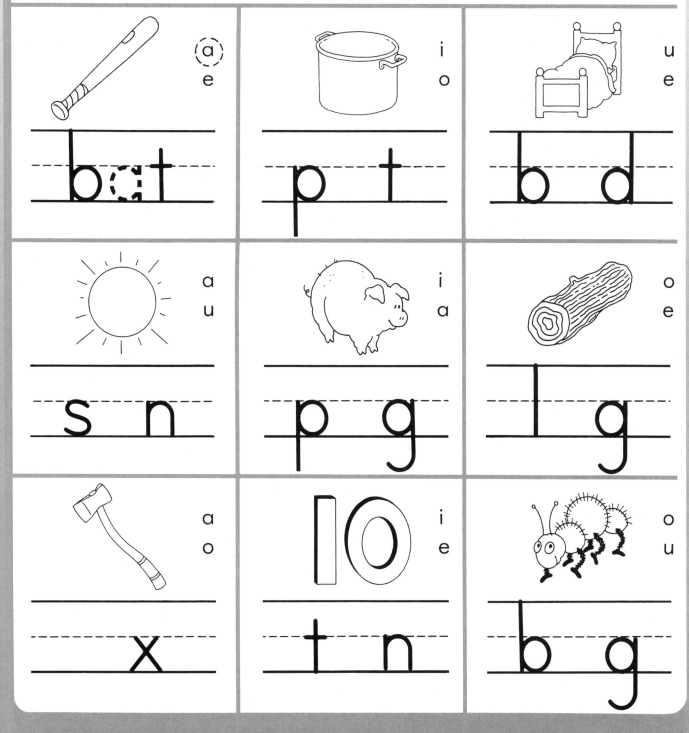

ⓐ e	i o	u e
b a t	p t	b d
a u	i a	o e
s n	p g	l g
a o	i e	o u
x	t n	b g

Short Vowels

Name _____

Circle the word that names each picture. Then write the word in the blank.

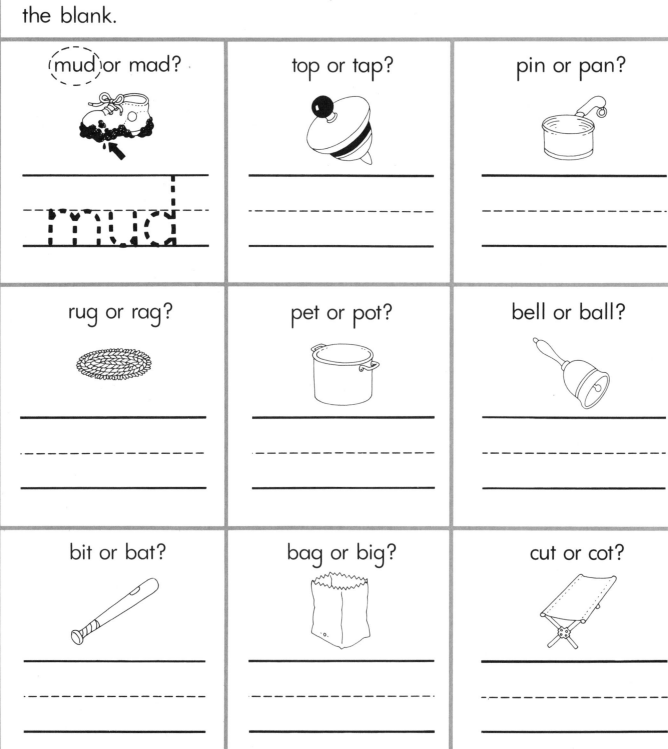

(mud) or mad?

mud

top or tap?

pin or pan?

rug or rag?

pet or pot?

bell or ball?

bit or bat?

bag or big?

cut or cot?

Symbol-sound association of short-vowel words: *a, e, i, o, u*

Short Vowels

Name _____

In each row, look at the letters and name the pictures. Circle each picture whose name has the short vowel sound the letter stands for.

a			
e			
i			
o			
u			

Short Vowels

Name _____

Name the pictures. Circle the letter that stands for the vowel sound in each picture name.

(i) a o u 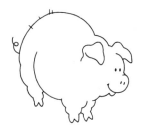	u e i a 	a o e i 
e u a o 	i o e u 	a e u i 
u e i o 	e a u o 	a i o u 
a e u o 	e o i u 	i a e o 

116

Sound-symbol association of short vowels: *a, e, i, o, u*

Short Vowels

Name _____

Read the sentences and the words under the blanks. Circle the word that belongs in each sentence. Then write the word in the blank.

1. Ted wants to make the _____ 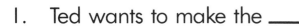.
   (bed) bad

2. The pig fell into the _____.
   mud   mad

3. The _____ is in a big box.
   hill   doll

4. Mom will make a bed for the _____.
   cats   cuts

5. The _____ ran into its den.
   fox   fix

6. Ana had on her tan _____.
   cub   cap

Short Vowels

Name

Read the words and look at the pictures. Draw a line from the pictures to the words they tell about.

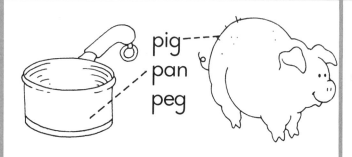

pig
pan
peg

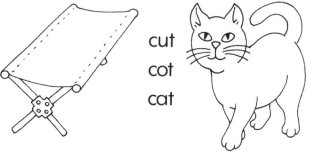

cut
cot
cat

fan
fin
fun

hat
hit
hut

bug
bag
beg

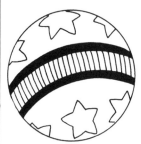

bell
bill
ball

wig
win
wag

zip
sip
rip

Symbol-sound association of short-vowel words: *a, e, i, o, u*

Short Vowels

Name _____

Read the sentences and the words under the blanks. Circle the word that belongs in each sentence. Then write the word in the blank.

1. Tim wants to play with the red _____.

(top) tap

2. Put the _____ on the _____.
   led   lid   pot   pat

3. Pam sees a doll on the _____.
   cut   cot

4. She hit the ball with the _____.
   bit   bat

5. The six _____ play in the _____.
   pigs   pegs   mad   mud

6. The bag had a blue _____ on it.
   tug   tag

Short Vowels

Name

Read the sentences and look at the pictures. Draw a line from each sentence to the picture it tells about.

The cat plays with the rag.
The cat plays with the rug.

Dad has the mop.
Dad has the map.

The dog has the bell.
The dog has the ball.

Lin got the bug.
Lin got the bag.

Dan has a red cup.
Dan has a red cap.

Mom will fix the ham.
Mom will fix the hem.

Short-vowel words in context

Short Vowels

Name _____

Look at each picture. Write the letter to complete the word that tells about the picture.

h a t

p _ t

w _ b

s _ n

s _ x

p _ g

b _ x

t _ g

h _ g

Long A

Rake has the long-**a** sound. This sound is often spelled by **a** and silent **e.**

r**a**k**e**

Name the pictures. Circle each picture whose name has the long-**a** sound.

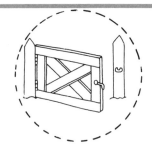   

 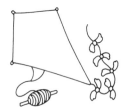 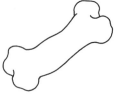 

Auditory discrimination of long *a*

Long A

Name _____

Name the pictures. Write the letter or letters to complete each picture name.

 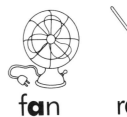

fan   **rake**

___ ___ ___

c a v e

c ___ ___ p

c ___ ___ p

l ___ ___ k

v ___ ___ s

f ___ ___ n

p ___ ___ n

b ___ ___ t

g ___ ___ t

Long A

Name_____

Read the words and name the pictures. Draw a line from each word to the picture it names.

fan   rake

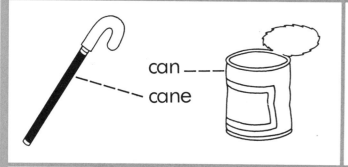

can
cane

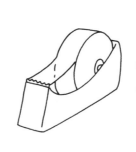 

ape
tape

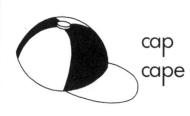

cap
cape

cave
cat

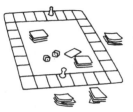

gate
game

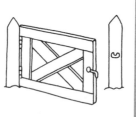

rake
lake

vase
wave

man
mane

Symbol-sound association of long-a words

Long A

Name _____

Read each sentence and words beside it. Write the word that makes sense in the sentence.

fan   **rake**

1. Dale __ate__ the ham.

at
ate
am

2. Is the _____ in the cave?

make
bat
mad

3. Mother wants to fix the _____.

get
gave
gate

4. Did you play the _____?

game
gate
gas

5. Jane will fix the pen with _____.

tape
tap
take

6. I have the _____ for the mix.

pan
rake
pat

Long *I*

Kite has the long-i sound. This sound is often spelled by **i** and silent **e**.

k**ite**

Name the pictures. Circle each picture whose name has the long-**i** sound.

Auditory discrimination of long i

Long *I*

Name _____

Read the words and look at the pictures. Draw a line from each word to the picture it tells about.

b**i**b   k**ite**

hive
five
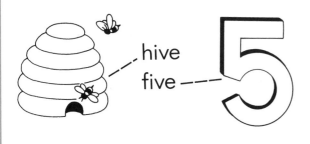

line
nine

bike
bite

tire
fire

kites
pipes
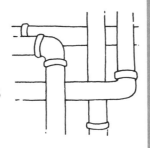

vine
pine

ride
wire

dive
dime

Long *I*

Name _____

Name the pictures. Write the letter or letters to complete each picture name.

bib   **kite**

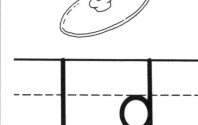

|ine

d___m

p___g

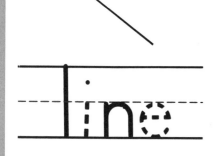

|___d

h___v

v___n

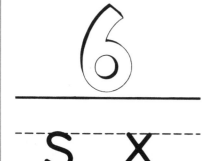

s___x

b___k

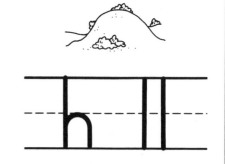

h___ll

Long *I*

Name _____

Read each sentence and the words beside it.
Write the word that makes sense in the sentence.

bib   **k*ite***

1. Jill will __*dive*__ into the lake.

did
dive
dime

2. Do you like to play with _____?

kit
kites
kiss

3. The _____ is in the pines.

hive
hid
hide

4. Kim will _____ the tire on the car.

fire
fix
file

5. I like to hike in the _____.

hive
hills
hid

6. Mike will _____ on his bike.

ripe
rid
ride

Long A and Long *I*

Read the words and look at the pictures. Circle the word that tells about each picture.

time tin tap (tape) 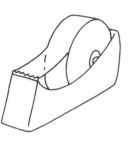	kit can kite cane 	dim dime date dam 
pan van vine pine 	bit bike bite big 	ride rat ran rid 
hide hive hat hate 	miss mat mitt man 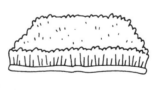	dive dad did date 
lad lid like lake 	sat side safe sit 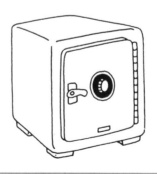	pine pin pal pale 

Review of symbol-sound association of long-*a* and long-*i* words

Long O

Name_____

Bone has the long-**o** sound. This sound is often spelled by **o** and silent **e**.

b**o**ne

Name the pictures. Circle each picture whose name has the long-**o** sound.

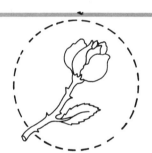   

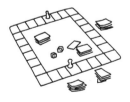 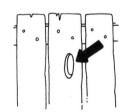  

   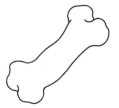

Auditory discrimination of long *o*

Long O

Read the words and look at the pictures.
Draw a line from each word to the picture
it tells about.

top

bone

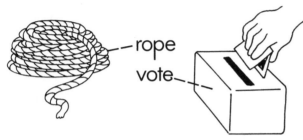
rope
vote

poke
pot

home
hop

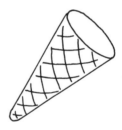
cone
bone

note
robe

hose
hole

pole
pop

rose
nose

Symbol-sound association of long-o words

Long O

Name the pictures. Write the letter or letters to complete each picture name.

 t**o**p   b**o**ne

n **o** t e

r ___ s

f ___ x

r ___ b

m ___ p

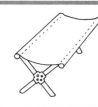

c ___ t

t ___ p

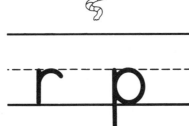

r ___ p

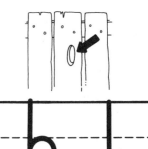

h ___ l

Long O

Name _____

Read each sentence and the words beside it. Write the word that makes sense in the sentence.

top   bone

1. Dad put the __rose__ into the vase.

rob
rose
nose

2. We hope you will tell us the _____.

joke
hop
poke

3. Tam _____ to the game with Lin.

rod
rope
rode

4. Rose put the red robe in a _____.

bone
box
mop

5. Did you _____ for Meg or Jan?

not
note
vote

6. Pam _____ the bone for Rags.

go
got
good

Long-o words in context

Long *U*

Tube has the long-**u** sound. This sound is often spelled by **u** and silent **e**.

tub**e**

Name the pictures. Circle each picture whose name has the long-**u** sound.

         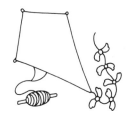

Auditory discrimination of long *u*

135

Long *U*

Name _____

Read the words and look at the pictures. Draw a line from each word to the picture it tells about.

cup   **tube**

mud
mule

rug
mug

cub
cube

run
ruler

cut
cute

tune
bun

tub
tube

bus
bug

Name _____

Look at each picture. Write the letter or letters to complete the word that tells about the picture.

c**u**p   t**u**be

m u | e

c | b

c | p

b | g

t | n

c | t

t | b

t | b

r | g

Long *U*

Name _____

Read each sentence and the words beside it.
Write the word that makes sense in the sentence.

cup   **tube**

1. Luke likes to ride on the _**mule**_ .

    mug
    mule
    mud

2. Can you play this _____?

    tub
    tune
    tube

3. I will use my dimes for the _____ ride.

    bus
    bug
    bun

4. Put the _____ in the cup.

    cub
    cute
    cube

5. I _____ my leg on the gate.

    cup
    cute
    cut

6. What are the _____ of the game?

    rugs
    rules
    rubs

Long-*u* words in context

Long O and Long U

Name _____

Read the words and name the pictures. Circle the word that names each picture.

cub cob cone (cube)	rode ruler rod run 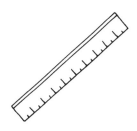	top toss tube tub 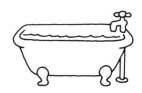
mop mug mole mule 	note nut not nose 	mule mug moss mole 
rule rose rod rug 	bone but bus box 	top tune tug tone 
rule run rope rot 	bone box bus bun 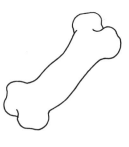	note nut nose not 

Review of symbol-sound association of long-o and long-u words

Long Vowels

Name _____

Name the pictures. Write the letters to complete each picture name.

 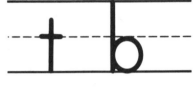 

h i v e   r _ _ p   t _ _ b

_ n _ t   m _ _ l   c _ b

b _ n   v _ n   _ _ k

  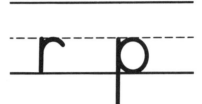

Review of sound-symbol association of long vowels

Long Vowels

Name _____

Read each sentence and the words beside it. Write the word that makes sense in the sentence.

1. Nine bats are in the __cave__.

cave
came
note

2. I may _____ a cape.

vote
make
kite

3. What is his _____?

name
five
nine

4. The lid is on the _____.

time
tune
tube

5. Did you _____ into the lake?

dive
hive
live

6. Muff wants to _____ the bone.

line
hope
hide

Long Vowels

Name _____

Circle the word that tells about each picture. Then write the word in the blank.

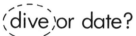 or date?

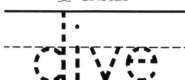

cube or cape?

_____

cone or cane?

_____

rode or rope?

_____

cute or cave?

_____

line or lake?

_____

rake or rope?

_____

time or tape?

_____

ride or rose?

_____

Symbol-sound association of long-vowel words

Long Vowels

Read the sentences and name the pictures. Write the word that names each picture.

1. It sounds like **line**.      It is a ___nine___.

2. It sounds like **name**.      It is a _____.

3. It sounds like **tube**.      It is a _____.

4. It sounds like **rake**.      It is a _____.

5. It sounds like **five**.   It is a _____.

6. It sounds like **cone**.      It is a _____.

Long Vowels

Name _____

Read the words below. Then name the pictures. Write the word that names each picture.

nine	tube	note
wave	rake	hive
bone	bike	cube

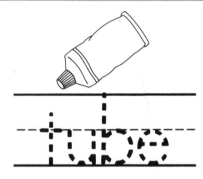

tube

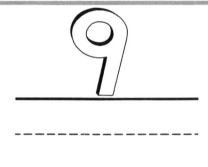

_____

_____

_____

_____

_____

_____

_____

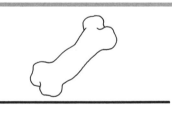

_____

Symbol-sound association of long-vowel words

Long Vowels

Name _____

Look at each picture. Circle the letters that stand for the vowel sound. Then write the letters to complete the word that tells about the picture.

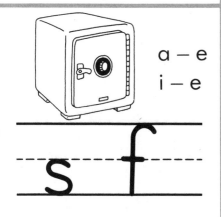 (a – e) o – e	 u – e i – e	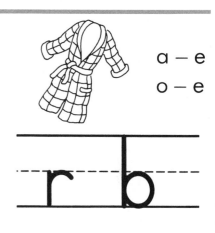 a – e o – e
r a k e	d _ v _	r _ b _
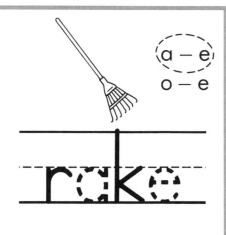 a – e i – e	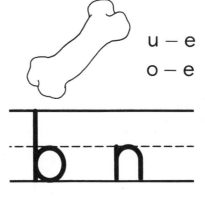 u – e o – e	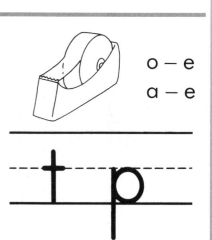 o – e a – e
s _ f _	b _ n _	t _ p _
 i – e a – e	 u – e o – e	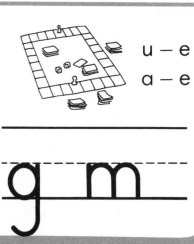 u – e a – e
b _ k _	m _ l _	g _ m _

Long Vowels

Read the sentences and look at the pictures. Draw a line from each sentence to the picture it tells about.

Todd rode the mule.
Todd rode the bike.

The rose is in the vase.
The vine is in the vase.

Rags has a bone.
Rags has a kite.

Pam plays a tune.
Pam plays a game.

The rope is on the bed.
The tube is on the bed.

Rose has on a cape.
Rose has on a robe.

Long-vowel words in context

Long Vowels

Name _____

Name the pictures. Write the letters to complete each picture name.

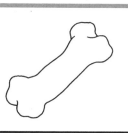

t u b e   c ___ p   b ___ n

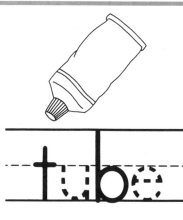

r ___ s   m ___ l   l ___ n

c ___ n   b ___ k   h ___ v

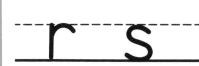

Sound-symbol association of long vowels

Long Vowels

Name _____

Read the words and name the pictures. Circle the word that names each picture.

(rope) rake rule ripe 	bone bake bite bike 	rose rise rake rope 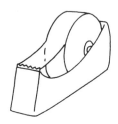
date dime dive dine 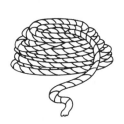	cube cone cove cane 	tape tube take tale 
take tube tore time 	wire wore vane vine 	tube tune tame tale 
name nine nose note 	rude ride rode ruler 	nose note name nine 

Symbol-sound association of long-vowel words

Long Vowels

Read the sentences and name the pictures. Write the word that names each picture.

1. It sounds like **nose.**      It is a .

2. It sounds like **late.**      It is a _____.

3. It sounds like **rule.**      It is a _____.

4. It sounds like **bake.**   It is a _____.

5. It sounds like **nine.**      It is a _____.

6. It sounds like **save.**      It is a _____.

PROGRESS CHECK

Long Vowels

Name _____

Name the pictures. Write the letters to complete each picture name.

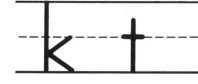

t u n e   n n   k t

I k   t p   r p

v n   m l   r b

Assessment of sound-symbol association of long vowels

Short and Long Vowels

Name _____

Name the pictures. Write the letter or letters to complete each picture name.

v i n e

r _ s _

_ l _ k

w _ b

f _ v _

f _ x

m _ l

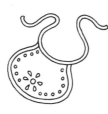

b _ b

_ t _ n

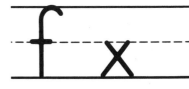

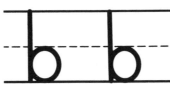

Sound-symbol association of short and long vowels

Short and Long Vowels

Name

Read the words and name the pictures. Draw lines from the words to the pictures they name.

pan
pale
pad

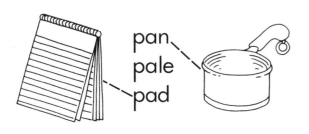

nose
not
note

cat
cave
came

rose
robe
rob

bike
bib
bite

cube
cut
cub

man
mane
map

pine
pig
pin

152

Short and Long Vowels

Name _____

Read each sentence and the words beside it. Write the word that makes sense in the sentence.

1. Did you ride the __bike__?

bit
bite
bike

2. Put on the red _____.

rob
rug
robe

3. Tell Jane to _____ the kite.

fix
fox
five

4. I have _____ dimes to save.

net
nine
name

5. The _____ ran into the den.

fat
fox
fine

6. Put the _____ on the pot.

lid
like
line

Short and Long Vowels

Name _____

Read the sentences and name the pictures. Write the word that names each picture.

1. It sounds like **bite.**  It is a  ____.

2. It sounds like **fan.**  It is a ____.

3. It sounds like **cot.** It is a ____.

4. It sounds like **red.**  It is a ____.

5. It sounds like **nose.**  It is a ____.

6. It sounds like **save.**  It is a ____.

Sound-symbol association of short- and long-vowel words

Short and Long Vowels

Name _____

Read the words below. Then name the pictures. Write the word that names each picture.

nine	rose	bat
pig	hive	cube
box	cane	sun

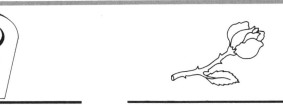

sun

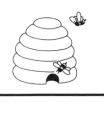 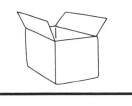 

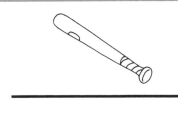  

Short and Long Vowels

Name _____

Read the sentences and look at the pictures. Draw a line from each sentence to the picture it tells about.

 The cap is on the bed.
The cape is on the bed.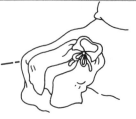

 Put the can in the box.
Put the cane in the box.

 Muff bats at the tub.
Muff bats at the tube.

 Mom has the kit.
Mom has the kite.

 Tam sees the cub.
Tam sees the cube.

 Let me take the tag.
Let me take the tape.

Short- and long-vowel words in context

Short and Long Vowels

Name _____

Name each picture. Write the letter or letters to complete the word that names the picture.

c a v e

l _ k

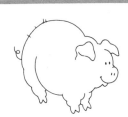

p _ g

j _ t

r _ p

n _ n

t _ b

s _ n

f _ n

S Blends

Name _____

In some words, the letter **s** comes before another consonant. To say these words, blend the sound of **s** with the sound of the consonant that follows it.

stop   **sk**ate
smile   **sl**eep

Look at the pictures. In each row, circle the picture or pictures that begin with the same sound as the first picture.

Auditory discrimination of initial s blends: *st, sm, sk, sl*

S Blends

Name _____

Read the words below. Then look at the pictures. Write the word that tells about each picture.

sled	skip	step	smoke	stem
skate	stone	slide	smile	

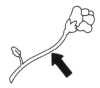

stem

_____

_____

_____

_____

_____

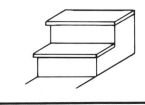

_____

_____

_____

S Blends

Name _____

Read each sentence and the words beside it. Write the word that makes sense in the sentence.

1. The ham __smells__ good.

smells
stops
slaps

2. The _____ slid down the hill.

slim
slot
sled

3. The rose _____ is green.

stem
skip
slip

4. The _____ stone hit the car.

sled
small
slam

5. Can you _____?

skip
stiff
slam

6. _____ at the red house.

Still
Stop
Slim

160

S Blends

Name _____

In some words, the letter **s** comes before another consonant. To say these words, blend the sound of **s** with the sound of the consonant that follows it.

scare	**sn**ap
swim	**sp**in

Look at the pictures. In each row, circle the picture or pictures that begin with the same sound as the first picture.

S Blends

Name _____

Read the words below. Then look at the pictures. Write the word that tells about each picture.

spill	snake	scale	snip	spell
snap	scare	swim	spin	

scare

_____

_____

_____

_____

_____

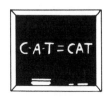

_____

_____

_____

Symbol-sound association of initial s-blend words: sc, sw, sn, sp

S Blends

Name _____

Read each sentence and the words beside it. Write the word that makes sense in the sentence.

1. Can you _____**swim**_____?

snake
swim
spoke

2. The _____ is in the hole.

snake
spell
snip

3. Jan can _____ well.

spell
snake
swam

4. Rose wants to _____ Jane.

spoke
swam
scare

5. I _____ to Stan and Skip.

snip
spill
spoke

6. Can the top _____?

scale
spin
spoke

S Blends

Read the words and look at the pictures. Circle the word that tells about each picture.

slim (skip) snip swim 	smell swell spell still 	spine smile skid slide 
spoke stone smoke slope 	swim slim spin skin 	stop slap skip snap 
spill swell smell still 	snake state scale spare 	spin skin slim swim 

Review of symbol-sound association of s-blend words: *st, sm, sk, sl, sc, sw, sn, sp*

L Blends

Name _____

In some words, the letter **l** follows another consonant. To say these words, blend the sound of the first consonant with the sound of **l.**

flower
play

Name the pictures. In each row, circle the picture or pictures that begin with the same sound as the first picture.

L Blends

Name _____

Read the words below. Then look at the pictures. Write the word that tells about each picture.

play	plate	flag	flute	plane
plug	flame	flat	plum	

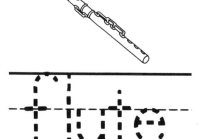

flute

_____

_____

_____

_____

_____

_____

_____

_____

Symbol-sound association of initial *l*-blend words: *fl, pl*

L Blends

Name _____

Read each sentence and the words beside it. Write the word that makes sense in the sentence.

1. The car has a __flat__ tire.

flip
flat
flame

2. Can you _____ the flute?

flat
play
plan

3. Mom got on the _____.

play
plug
plane

4. The _____ has a rip.

flame
flag
flat

5. The _____ is hot.

flame
plan
play

6. Can you do a _____?

flip
flat
flag

Words containing initial *l* blends in context: *fl, pl*

167

L Blends

Name _____

In some words, the letter **l** follows another consonant. To say these words, blend the sound of the first consonant with the sound of **l**.

clown
blue
glad

Look at the pictures. In each row, circle the picture or pictures that begin with the same sound as the first picture.

 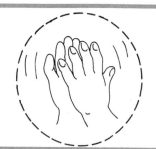  

   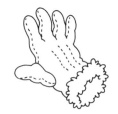

Auditory discrimination of initial *l* blends: *cl, bl, gl*

L Blends

Name _____

Read the words below. Then look at the pictures. Write the word that tells about each picture.

clip	blade	globe	clam	glass
club	clap	class	glad	

_____ club _____   _____   _____

_____   _____   _____

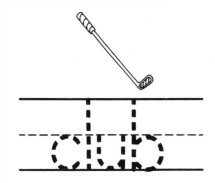

_____   _____   _____

L Blends

Name _____

Read each sentence and the words beside it. Write the word that makes sense in the sentence.

1. Will Glenn go with the __class__ ?

clap
class
clip

2. The _____ had ice in it.

glass
glad
class

3. Do you like the _____ cap?

clap
clam
blue

4. Do not _____ Tam for the mess.

blaze
blame
blade

5. Pablo is _____ he got a dog.

globe
glass
glad

6. The _____ met at my house.

clam
club
clip

Words containing initial *l* blends in context: *cl, bl, gl*

L Blends

Name _____

Read the words and name the pictures. Circle the word that names each picture.

(clip) flap glad plan 	clap blaze glass flame 	flute plate blade glad 
glare plane flame blade 	plane flake blame clam 	play clap flag glad 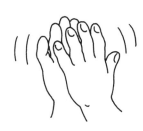
club plug flag glad 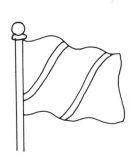	flake plate blame glare 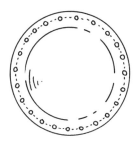	globe blob club plug 

R Blends

Name _____

In some words, the letter **r** follows another consonant. To say these words, blend the sound of the first consonant with the sound of **r.**

frog
brown
green

Name the pictures. In each row, circle the pictures that begin with the same sound as the first picture.

Auditory discrimination of initial *r* blends: *fr, br, gr*

R Blends

Name _____

Read the words below. Then look at the pictures. Write the word that tells about each picture.

grab	frog	bride	grade	grape
grill	grin	frame	graze	

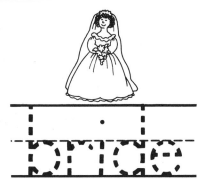

bride

_____

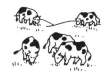

_____

_____

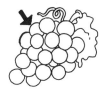

_____

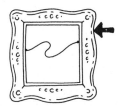

_____

_____

_____

_____

R Blends

Name _____

Read each sentence and the words beside it. Write the word that makes sense in the sentence.

1. Greg gave me a red __frame__ .

   frame
   broke
   froze

2. The _____ hops on the log.

   grip
   frog
   broke

3. Fran will _____ the rope.

   grape
   grab
   from

4. Fred likes _____ jam.

   grape
   grade
   grab

5. The _____ is hot.

   grin
   grill
   grade

6. Did you see the _____?

   graze
   from
   bride

Words containing initial *r* blends in context: *fr, br, gr*

R Blends

Name _____

In some words, the letter **r** follows another consonant. To say these words, blend the sound of the first consonant with the sound of **r.**

cry   **pr**etty
dress   **tr**ee

Look at the pictures. In each row, circle the picture or pictures that begin with the same sound as the first picture.

Auditory discrimination of initial r blends: *cr, dr, pr, tr*

175

R Blends

Name_____

Read the words below. Then look at the pictures. Write the word that tells about each picture.

trip	trap	crib	drip	crab
dress	drill	drum	prize	

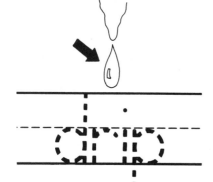

_____

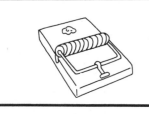

_____

_____

Symbol-sound association of initial r-blend words: cr, dr, pr, tr

R Blends

Name _____

Read each sentence and the words beside it. Write the word that makes sense in the sentence.

1. Did you __drive__ to the house?

drive
drill
drop

2. What was the _____?

trot
drag
prize

3. Fran likes to play the _____.

drum
crib
prize

4. Did Kris _____ the hot pan?

drum
drive
drop

5. Do not grab the _____.

trip
crab
trot

6. Did you _____ on the crate?

trap
crib
trip

Words containing initial *r* blends in context: *cr, dr, pr, tr*

177

R Blends

Name _____

Read the words and look at the pictures. Circle the word that tells about each picture.

(grapes) brave trade frames 	from drum grab crate 	grill drip crib trap 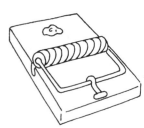
crab grass trap drag 	prize bride drive trade 	drag frog crop grab 
prize bride froze drive 	grin trim drum from 	graze prize prune bride 

Review of symbol-sound association of initial *r*-blend words: *fr, br, gr, cr, dr, pr, tr*

Final S Blends

Name _____

At the end of some words, the letter **s** comes before another consonant. To say these words, blend the sound of **s** with the sound of that consonant.

a**sk**

ju**st**

Look at the pictures. In each row, circle the picture or pictures that end with the same sound as the first picture.

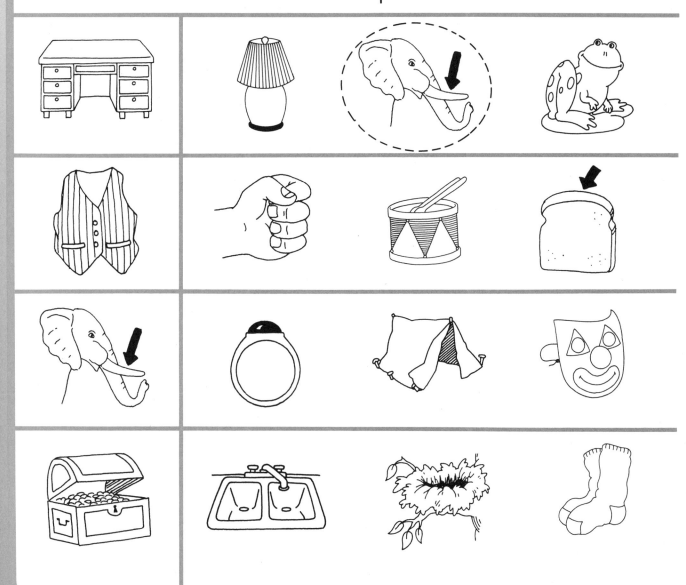

Final *S* Blends

Name _____

Read the words below. Then look at the pictures. Write the word that tells about each picture.

list	nest	fist
mask	cast	desk
crust	vest	tusk

 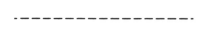 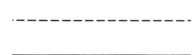

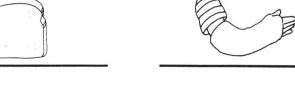 _____ _____

_____ _____ _____

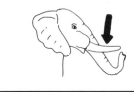  

_____ _____ _____

Symbol-sound association of final *s*-blend words: *st, sk*

Final S Blends

Name _____

Read each sentence and the words beside it. Write the word that makes sense in the sentence.

1. Please _____ask_____ for help.

    mask
    ask
    most

2. I _____ my hat.

    lost
    list
    last

3. A pen is in the _____.

    dust
    desk
    mask

4. Sam hit the ball with his _____.

    fast
    list
    fist

5. What is the _____ of the toy?

    crust
    cost
    cast

6. Do you have a red _____?

    best
    vest
    last

Words containing final s blends in context: st, sk

Read the words and look at the pictures. Circle the word that tells about each picture.

test nest task (tusk) 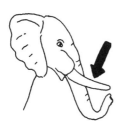	cast crust dust desk 	list last test tusk eggs ham milk
cost cast mask most 	pest nest must mask 	most desk dust mask 
tusk test vest most 	desk ask mask must 	fast task fist tusk 

Review of symbol-sound association of final s-blend words: st, sk

Blends

Name _____

Read the words below. Then look at the pictures. Write the word that tells about each picture.

drum	sled	desk	flag	snake
crab	nest	plate	frog	

crab

Vowel Pairs: *AI* and *AY*

Name _____

Train has the long-**a** sound spelled **ai**. **Hay** has the long-**a** sound spelled **ay**.

tr**ai**n   h**ay**

Read the words and look at the pictures. Circle the word that tells about each picture.

(rain) / ray	train / tray	mail / nail
sail / say	plain / play	mail / may
snail / sail	tray / trail	brain / braid
rail / ray	tail / trail	claim / clay

Symbol-sound association of words containing vowel digraphs: *ai, ay*

Vowel Pairs: *AI* and *AY*

Name _____

Read each sentence and the words beside it. Write the word that makes sense in the sentence.

train   **hay**

1. The dog wags its ___tail___.

   tail
   trail
   train

2. My house has a gray _____.

   ray
   rail
   raise

3. Put the glass on the _____.

   tray
   tail
   train

4. Tam likes to _____.

   sail
   say
   snail

5. Do you like to _____ with clay?

   plain
   pain
   play

6. A snail is in the _____.

   pay
   pain
   pail

Vowel Pairs: *AI* and *AY*

Name _____

Read the sentences and the list of words. Write the word from the list that makes sense in each sentence.

 train

 **hay**

1. The _____ **maid** _____ made the bed.

2. I hope it will not _____.

3. The class takes a hike on the _____.

4. Use ten _____ to make the frame.

5. We _____ see the play.

6. The vase is made of _____.

rain
clay
may
nails
maid
trail

Words containing vowel digraphs in context: *ai, ay*

Vowel Pairs: *EE* and *EA*

Bee has the long-**e** sound spelled **ee**. **Bean** has the long-**e** sound spelled **ea**.

b**ee**   b**ea**n

Read the words and look at the pictures. Circle the word that tells about each picture.

see
(seat)

meat
neat

sea
seal

feet
fee

beak
bee

sleep
seat

tea
team

bee
beef

jeep
jeans

peas
peel

heat
heel

leap
leaf

Vowel Pairs: *EE* and *EA*

Name_____

Read each sentence and the words beside it.
Write the word that makes sense in the sentence.

bee   **bean**

1. Please save me a ___seat___ at the game.

    sea
    seat
    seem

2. Lee will ride in the _____.

    jeep
    green
    sleep

3. The _____ is on the rose.

    beef
    beat
    bee

4. Jean wants to be on the _____.

    neat
    team
    see

5. Dean put _____ on his plate.

    need
    peas
    neat

6. It is fun to see the _____.

    peels
    real
    seals

Words containing vowel digraphs in context: *ee, ea*

Vowel Pairs: *EE* and *EA*

Name _____

Read the sentences and the list of words. Write the word from the list that makes sense in each sentence.

b**ee**   b**ea**n

1. Dee will __**need**__ a hat.

2. Do you want to eat the _____?

3. The _____ will be cut down.

4. The grass feels good on my _____.

5. Neal keeps his home _____.

6. The _____ is deep and blue.

neat
need
sea
tree
meat
feet

AI, AY, EE, and EA

Name_____

Read the words and look at the pictures. Circle the word that tells about each picture.

sail say (seal) see 	pay pail peel peas 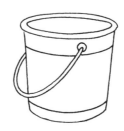	bee beat beak beef 
tail team tea tray 	mail may meat meet 	ray rain read real 
play pay pain pail 	train tray rain tree 	hay heat heel hail 

Review of symbol-sound association of words containing vowel digraphs: *ai, ay, ee, ea*

Vowel Pairs: OA and OW

Name _____

Coat has the long-**o** sound spelled **oa**.

Window has the long-**o** sound spelled **ow**.

c**oa**t   wind**ow**

Read the words and look at the pictures. Circle the word that tells about each picture.

boat (bowl) 	snow soap 	goat grow 
crow coat	row road 	float flow 
blow bow 	tow toad 	crow coal 
load low 	slow snow 	oak oats 

Vowel Pairs: OA and OW

Name _____

Read each sentence and the words beside it. Write the word that makes sense in the sentence.

coat

window

1. May I please **row** the boat?

goat
row
oak

2. Feed the oats to the _____.

snow
goat
bow

3. My _____ has a hole in it.

snow
load
coat

4. The _____ sat on a leaf.

bow
toad
row

5. Mother wants to _____ the car.

low
loaf
load

6. Jeff put the peas into a _____.

snow
bowl
soap

Words containing vowel digraphs in context: oa, ow

Vowel Pairs: OA and OW

Name _____

Read the sentences and the list of words. Write the word from the list that makes sense in each sentence.

c**oa**t   wind**ow**

1. The _____ is in the bay.

2. I will use _____ to clean the car.

3. Did the rose _____ well?

4. The _____ ate the beans.

5. The _____ fell on the housetops.

6. A red _____ is on the box.

boat
snow
bow
grow
soap
crows

Vowel Pairs: oo

Name _____

The sound you hear in the middle of **moon** is spelled by the letters **oo**.

m**oo**n

Name the pictures. Write **oo** below each picture whose name has the **oo** sound as in **moon.**

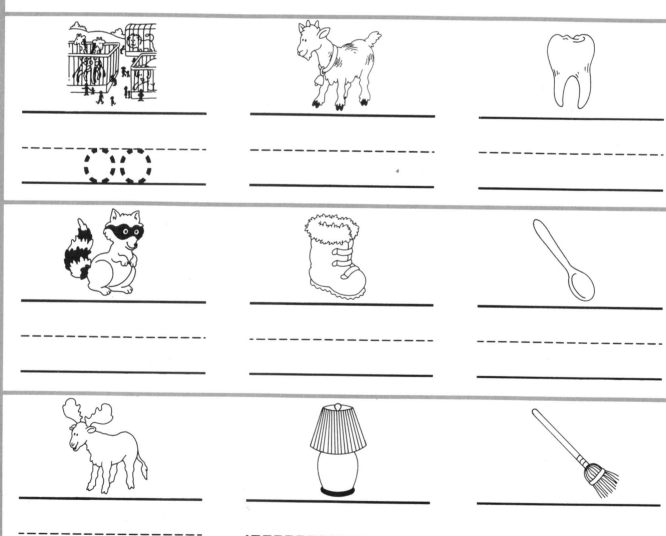

Vowel Pairs: OO

Name_____

The sound you hear in the middle of **book** is spelled by the letters **oo**.

book

Name the pictures. Write **oo** below each picture whose name has the **oo** sound as in **book.**

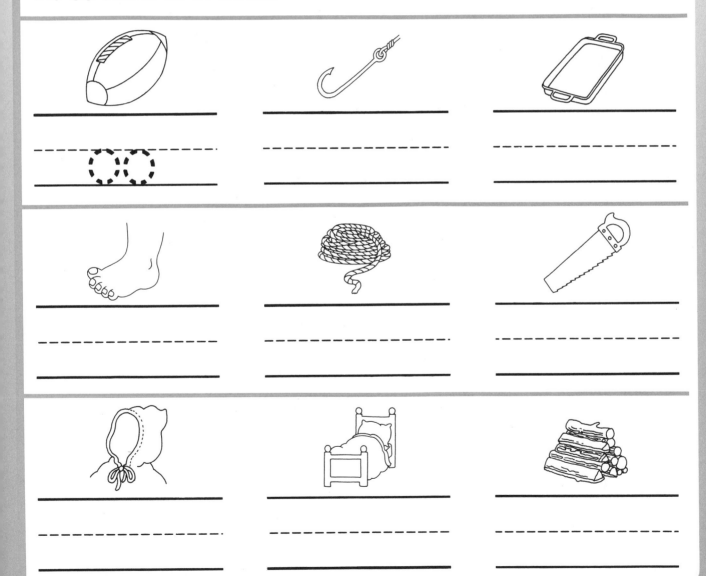

Vowel Pairs: OO

Name_____

Read the words and name the pictures. Draw a line from each word to the picture it names.

m**oo**n   b**oo**k

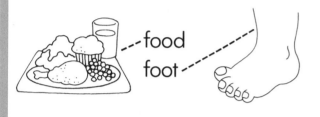 food
foot

 pool
roof

 zoo
woods

moose
hood

book
boot

spoon
spool

hook
stool

broom
brook

Symbol-sound association of words containing vowel digraphs: long and short *oo*

OA, OW, and OO

Read the words and name the pictures. Circle the word that names each picture.

book (boat) boot bowl 	foot float flow foam 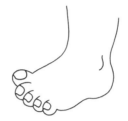	stool stood soap snow 
grow good goat goal 	low look load loaf 	crow cool coal cook 
tool took tow toad 	bow blow broom book 	slow stoop soap spoon 

Review of symbol-sound association of words containing vowel digraphs: *oa, ow, oo*

A Sound of Y

Name _____

The letter **y** at the end of some words can stand for the long-**i** sound, as in **fly**.

fl**y**

Name the pictures. Write **y** below each picture whose name has the long-**i** sound, as in **fly**.

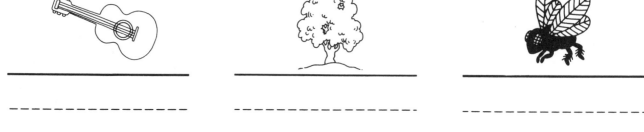

Sound-symbol association of words containing the long-*i* sound of *y*

A Sound of Y

Name_____

The letter **y** at the end of some words can stand for the long-**e** sound, as in **pony.**

po**ny**

Name the pictures. Write **y** below each picture whose name has the long-**e** sound, as in **pony.**

_____

y

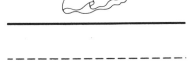

Two Sounds of Y

Name _____

Read the words and look at the pictures. Circle the word that tells about each picture.

fl**y**   pon**y**

pretty
(penny)
pry

fly
funny
fry

try
fry
cry

sly
spy
sky

pry
puppy
pony

by
baby
bunny

pry
fry
try

by
bye
baby

pony
penny
puppy

Symbol-sound association of words containing long-*e* and long-*i* sounds of *y*

Two Sounds of Y

Name _____

Read each sentence and the words beside it. Write the word that makes sense in each sentence.

fl**y**   pon**y**

1. The _**sky**_ is blue.	by sky try
2. Put the _____ in the crib.	baby by dry
3. Do you want to _____ a plane?	pony sky fly
4. The name of the _____ is Tommy.	penny puppy pretty
5. Jimmy will _____ the eggs.	fly fry funny
6. I lost my _____ in this room.	penny pretty happy

Vowel Pairs and Sounds of Y

Name _____

Read the words and name the picture. Circle the word that names each picture.

(mail) mow 	snail snow 	try tray 
see seal 	bee by 	boat book 
soap seem 	bait boot 	hair hook 
bunny bean 	stay sky 	baby by 

202

Assessment of sound-symbol association of words containing y as a vowel and of words containing vowel digraphs: ai, ay, ee, ea, oa, ow, oo

Consonant Pairs: *SH* and *CH*

Name _____

The sound at the beginning of **shoe** is spelled by the letters **sh.** The sound at the beginning of **chair** is spelled by the letters **ch.**

shoe   **ch**air

Name the pictures. In each row, circle the picture or pictures that begin with the same sound as the first picture.

Consonant Pairs: SH and CH

Name _____

Read the words below and look at the pictures.
Write the word that tells about each picture.

ship	shave	chain
sheep	chop	chin
cheek	shell	shed

shoe **ch**air

chain

_____ _____ _____

_____ _____ _____

_____ _____ _____

Consonant Pairs: *SH* and *CH*

Name _____

Read each sentence and the words beside it.
Write the word that makes sense in the sentence.

shoe   **ch**air

1. The ball hit Tony on the _____chin_____.	chain chin sheep
2. Did you _____ the wood?	chop shed chin
3. He has a red spot on his _____.	chain cheek cheese
4. The _____ ate the grass.	sheep shed shave
5. Put the bike in the _____.	chop shed cheek
6. Did Dad see this pretty _____?	shave shame shell

Consonant Pairs: *TH* and *WH*

Name _____

The sound at the beginning of **thin** is spelled by the letters **th.** The sound at the beginning of **wheel** is spelled by the letters **wh.**

thin   **wh**eel

Name the pictures. In each row, circle the picture or pictures that begin with the same sound as the first picture.

Auditory discrimination of initial consonant digraphs: *th, wh*

Consonant Pairs: *TH* and *WH*

Name_____

Name the pictures. Write the letters that stand for the beginning sound of each picture name.

thin **wh**eel

_____
wh
_____

_____
_ _ _ _ _ _ _ _
_____

_____
_ _ _ _ _ _ _ _
_____

_____
_ _ _ _ _ _ _ _
_____

_____
_ _ _ _ _ _ _ _
_____

_____
_ _ _ _ _ _ _ _
_____

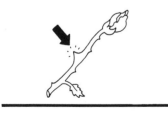

_____
_ _ _ _ _ _ _ _
_____

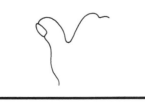

_____
_ _ _ _ _ _ _ _
_____

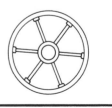

_____
_ _ _ _ _ _ _ _
_____

Consonant Pairs: *TH* and *WH*

Name _____

Read each sentence and the words beside it.
Write the word that makes sense in the sentence.

thin   **wh**eel

1. _____What_____ do you want to eat?

    Them
    What
    That

2. The _____ snow is on the trees.

    what
    wheat
    white

3. The cat is too _____.

    wheat
    why
    thin

4. _____ is a fine play.

    Them
    Whale
    This

5. _____ did you stay late?

    This
    Why
    That

6. Tell me _____ you can go.

    whip
    when
    what

Words containing initial consonant digraphs in context: *th, wh*

Consonant Pairs: Final *SH*, *CH*, and *TH*

Name _____

The sound at the end of **wish** is spelled by the letters **sh**.	wi**sh**
The sound at the end of **each** is spelled by the letters **ch**.	ea**ch**
The sound at the end of **with** is spelled by the letters **th**.	wi**th**

Name the pictures. In each row, circle the picture or pictures that end with the same sound as the first picture.

Consonant Pairs: Final *SH*, *CH*, and *TH*

Name _____

Name the pictures. Write the letters that stand for the end sound of each picture name.

wi**sh**
ea**ch**
wi**th**

_____

- - - - - - - - - -

_____

_____

- - - - - - - - - -

_____

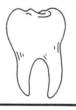

_____

- - - - - - - - - -

_____

_____

- - - - - - - - - -

_____

_____

- - - - - - - - - -

_____

_____

- - - - - - - - - -

_____

_____

- - - - - - - - - -

_____

_____

- - - - - - - - - -

_____

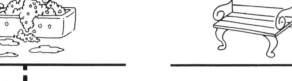

Sound-symbol association of final consonant digraphs: *sh, ch,* and *th*

Consonant Pairs: Final *SH, CH,* and *TH*

Name _____

Read each sentence and the words beside it. Write the word that makes sense in the sentence.	wi**sh** ea**ch** wi**th**

1. Did Pablo brush his __teeth__?

   dish
   math
   teeth

2. I will _____ my face.

   bush
   trash
   wash

3. We swim at the _____.

   peach
   beach
   reach

4. Eva ate a _____.

   sandwich
   leash
   inch

5. I gave the dog a _____.

   math
   path
   bath

6. I broke the blue _____.

   fish
   wish
   dish

Consonant Pairs: NG

The sound at the end of **ring** is spelled by the letters **ng.**

ri**ng**

Name the pictures. Circle each picture whose name ends with **ng.**

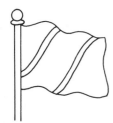   

Auditory discrimination of final consonant digraph: ng

Consonant Pairs: NG

Name _____

Read the words and look at the pictures. Circle the word that tells about each picture.

ri**ng**

(swing) sing 	wing sing 	bang hang 
sting king 	sting swing 	sing bring
song ring 	wing sting 	ring king

Consonant Pairs: *NG*

Name_____

Read each sentence and the words beside it.
Write the word that makes sense in the sentence.

ri**ng**

1. Did the bee ___**sting**___ you?	ring sting sing
2. Can you _____ this tune?	song sing king
3. The _____ has a ring.	king sting sing
4. The jay had blue _____.	wings kings sings
5. Did you drop the _____?	sing ring bring
6. I will _____ the drapes.	king rang hang

Name _____

Read the words and look at the pictures. Circle the word that tells about each picture.

(wing) sing bring ring 	chain when then shape 	chin thin whip ship 
math bath with path 	fish dish wash push 	whale shave cheese these 
inch each bench beach 	sheep cheap wheat that 	ring wing sing swing 

Review of symbol-sound association of words containing consonant
digraphs: initial *sh, ch, th, wh*, final *ch, sh, th, ng*

215

SH, CH, TH, WH, and NG

Name _____

Read the words below. Then look at the pictures. Write the word that tells about each picture.

ship	chain	thin	swing	shell
bench	wheel	brush	tooth	

chain

Assessment of symbol-sound association of words containing
consonant digraphs: initial *sh, ch, th, wh*, final *sh, ch, th, ng*

Endings: *-ED* and *-ING*

Name _____

Many words can be formed by adding **-ed** or **-ing** to other words.	play play**ed** play**ing**

Read the words below. Add **-ed** and **-ing** to each word to form new words. Write the new words in the blanks.

		Add **-ed**	Add **-ing**
1.	wait	waited	waiting
2.	look		
3.	toss		
4.	want		
5.	work		
6.	jump		

Base Words and Endings: *-ED* and *-ING*

Name _____

| A word to which an ending can be added is called a base word. The base word of **played** is **play.** The base word of **playing** is **play.** | **play**
 played
 playing |

Read each word below and write its base word.

1. needed ___need___

2. singing _____

3. passing _____

4. cleaned _____

5. loaded _____

6. glowing _____

7. filled _____

8. staying _____

9. jumped _____

10. spilling _____

11. floating _____

12. raining _____

Identifying base words

Endings: *-ED* and *-ING*

Name _____

Read each sentence and the words beside it. Write the word that makes sense in each sentence.

1. We __worked__ at the shop. worked / working

2. Tam _____ the shop. passed / passing

3. Is Grace _____ for a hat? looked / looking

4. Tony _____ for his mom. waited / waiting

5. Bob is _____ the ball. tossed / tossing

6. Rosa is _____ Kim. helped / helping

7. Max _____ to go home. wanted / wanting

-ED and -ING

Name _____

Read each sentence and the word beside it. Add **-ed** or **-ing** to the word so it makes sense in the sentence. Write the word in the blank.

1. Dan _____called_____ to his mom. call

2. The boat is _____ in the lake. float

3. Ramona is _____ us to go. tell

4. Dad _____ the room well. clean

5. The class will be _____ slides. show

6. We _____ at the shop. work

Review of using context clues to add -ed and -ing to verbs

-ED and -ING

Name _____

Read each sentence and the endings beside it. Add one of the endings to the word shown below the blank. Write the word in the blank to complete the sentence.

1. Pat __**waited**__ ten days for the books.
    (wait)
    -ed
    -ing

2. Kim is _____ for the boots.
    (look)
    -ed
    -ing

3. The frog _____ onto the log.
    (jump)
    -ed
    -ing

4. Jimmy will be _____ his room.
    (clean)
    -ed
    -ing

5. The puppy _____ to eat.
    (want)
    -ed
    -ing

6. Will you be _____ late?
    (stay)
    -ed
    -ing

Plurals: -S

Name _____

You can make many words mean "more than one" by adding **-s** to base words.

car   car**s**

Look at the pictures and read the words. Circle the word that names the picture or pictures in each box.

	hen (hens)		coat coats
	cat cats		hat hats
	bike bikes		tree trees
	fan fans		kite kites

222

Identifying singular and plural forms

Plurals: -S and -ES

Name _____

You can make some words mean "more than one" by adding **-s** to base words. When a word ends in **s, ss, sh, ch,** or **x,** add **-es** to make it mean "more than one."

top**s**	dish**es**
ax**es**	lunch**es**
bus**es**	dress**es**

Read the words below. Add **-s** or **-es** to each word to make it mean "more than one."

1. box _boxes_

2. bus _____

3. bush _____

4. can _____

5. glass _____

6. hat _____

7. inch _____

8. mix _____

9. tree _____

10. wish _____

Plurals: -S and -ES

Name _____

Read each sentence and the words beside it. Add **-s** or **-es** to one of the words so it makes sense in the sentence. Write the word in the blank.

1. The _____foxes_____ played in the den.

box
fox

2. Put the _____ on the rug.

boot
pool

3. Dad got five cake _____.

six
mix

4. The king gave away his _____.

rich
much

5. Did you trim the _____?

bush
rash

6. _____ like to eat grass.

Boat
Goat

Plurals: -S and -ES

Name _____

Read each sentence and the words beside it. Add **-s** or **-es** to one of the words so it makes sense in the sentence. Write the word in the blank.

1. The oak ___trees___ had to be cut.

    pen
    tree

2. The _____ ran by the lake.

    fox
    box

3. Jimmy made the _____.

    lunch
    much

4. Put five _____ into this bag.

    can
    wish

5. Mike fell into the rose _____.

    frame
    bush

6. Did you use _____ in the cake mix?

    hat
    egg

Plurals

Name _____

Read the words below. Add **-s** or **-es** to each word to make it mean "more than one."

1. hen hens

2. mix _____

3. lunch _____

4. class _____

5. coat _____

6. dish _____

7. wish _____

8. bus _____

9. song _____

10. bird _____

11. glass _____

12. rich _____

Review of adding -s or -es to form plurals

Plurals

Name _____

Read each sentence and the endings beside it. Add one of the endings to the word shown below the blank. Write the word in the blank to complete the sentence.

1. Put the __boxes__ in the den.
   (box)
   -s
   -es

2. Gail made five _____.
   (wish)
   -s
   -es

3. Will you make the _____?
   (bed)
   -s
   -es

4. All of the _____ will stop here.
   (bus)
   -s
   -es

5. Take the _____ off the stove.
   (pan)
   -s
   -es

6. All of the _____ will go to the zoo.
   (class)
   -s
   -es

Contractions

Name_____

A contraction is a short way to write two words. It is written by putting two words together and leaving out a letter or letters. An apostrophe (') takes the place of the letter or letters that are left out.

did + not = **didn't**

I + am = **I'm**

Read the list of words below. Then read the word pairs that follow. Write a contraction from the list for each word pair.

aren't   I'm   isn't   haven't

doesn't   hasn't   wasn't   didn't

1. have not

2. was not _____

3. I am _____

4. does not _____

5. are not _____

6. is not _____

7. did not _____

8. has not _____

Forming contractions using *not, am*

Contractions

Read each contraction below. Then write the two words for which each contraction stands.

I + will = **I'll**
it + is = **it's**

1. she'll _____ _____

2. he's _____ _____

3. we'll _____ _____

4. he'll _____ _____

5. it's _____ _____

6. I'll _____ _____

7. she's _____ _____

Recognizing words within contractions using *will* and *is*

Contractions

Name _____

Read each sentence below. Write the contraction for the words shown below the blank in each sentence.

1. **She's** _____ glad to see us.
   (She is)

2. _____ jumping up and down.
   (I am)

3. _____ play ball with you.
   (I will)

4. He _____ late for work.
   (is not)

5. _____ easy to make lunch.
   (It is)

6. They _____ go to the picnic.
   (did not)

Forming contractions in context, using *not, am, will, is*

Contractions

Name _____

Read each sentence below. Write the contraction for the words shown below the blank in each sentence.

1. _____ clean my room.
   (I will)

2. Ramona _____ asked to sing.
   (was not)

3. _____ glad to meet you.
   (I am)

4. The meat _____ smell good.
   (did not)

5. _____ fun to ride a bike.
   (It is)

6. Jim did not say _____ funny.
   (he is)

Contractions

Name _____

Read each pair of words below. Write the contraction for each word pair.

1. is not _____isn't_____

2. she is _____

3. I will _____

4. he is _____

5. was not _____

6. we will _____

7. it is _____

8. I am _____

9. he will _____

10. did not _____

11. are not _____

12. does not _____

Assessment of forming contractions

Name _____

Each letter has its own place in the alphabet.

a b c d e f g h i j k l m
n o p q r s t u v w x y z

Look at the letters in each box. In the blank, write the missing letter.
The letters in each box should be in ABC order.

m __ o __   __ u __ w

__ b __ d   c __ e __

__ x y __   __ p __ r __

j __ l __   __ __ __ h i

ABC Order

Name _____

a b c d e f g h i j k l m
n o p q r s t u v w x y z

Look at the letters in each box. Write the letters in ABC order.

mkl __k l m__

poq _____

pon _____

srq _____

ghf _____

cba _____

zyx _____

hji _____

ABC Order

a b c d e f g h i j k l m
n o p q r s t u v w x y z

Look at the letters in each box. Write the letters in ABC order. The letters you write should form a word.

opm _mop_	edn _____
tih _____	ebg _____
bte _____	fyl _____
ofx _____	ton _____

Arranging letters in alphabetical order to form words

235

ABC Order

Name _____

Write the missing letters to complete the alphabet.

a b   __ e

__ g h __ j

__ l m __ __

p __ r __ t

__ v __ y __

Review of supplying missing letters of the alphabet.

ABC Order

Name _____

Look at the letters in each box. Write the letters in ABC order. The letters you write should form a word.

onw ___now___	obx _____
tif _____	cto _____
tbi _____	mih _____
ogt _____	fni _____

Sounds and Letters

fa**n**

ra**ke**

trai**n**

hay

ball

car

chair

dog

be**d**

bea**n**

bee

fish

goat

horse

bi**b**

Sounds and Letters

 **k**ite

 **j**et

 **k**itten

 **l**ion

 **m**ouse

 **n**est

 ri**ng**

 **t**op

 c**oa**t

 b**one**

 m**oo**n

 b**oo**k

 wind**ow**

 pig

quilt

Sounds and Letters

 **r**ose

 **s**un

 **sh**oe

 **t**ent

 thin

 c**u**p

 t**u**b**e**

 vase

 **w**atch

 wheel

 a**x**

 **y**ard

 fl**y**

 pon**y**

 **z**oo

Matching Letters

Name_____

In each row, circle the letter that is the same as the first letter in the row.

G	O	R	(G)	B
M	T	P	Y	(M)
R	N	B	(R)	I
B	(B)	O	Y	P
W	A	M	(W)	B
J	U	C	(J)	B
T	(T)	I	L	E

Matching Letters

Name_____

In each row, circle the letter that is the same as the first letter in the row.

a	m	(a)	h	c
d	t	o	(d)	r
k	w	d	t	(k)
f	h	t	p	(f)
q	(q)	o	g	m
c	o	z	(c)	g
s	w	(s)	m	a

Recognizing Letters

Name_____

All letters of the alphabet can be written in capital and small letters. Example: **N n.** In each row, circle the letters that belong with the first letter in the row.

S	p	(s)	t	(s)
f	T	O	(F)	(F)
j	(J)	G	O	(J)
O	b	(o)	(o)	m
P	(p)	s	t	(p)
I	z	(i)	t	(i)
m	A	(M)	N	(M)

Recognizing Letters

Name_____

All letters of the alphabet can be written in capital and small letters. Example: **I i.** In each row, circle the letters that belong with the first letter in the row.

c	(C)	L	(C)	O
K	(k)	p	h	(k)
t	N	(T)	(T)	Z
Y	(y)	(y)	z	f
U	(u)	o	(u)	n
W	t	(w)	u	(w)
v	(V)	A	B	(V)

Beginning Sounds

Name_____

Name the pictures. In each row, circle the pictures that begin with the same sound as the first picture in the row.

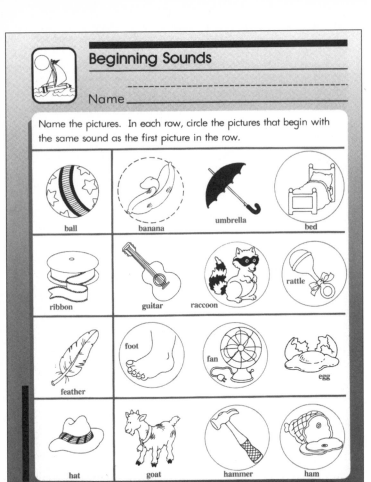

ball · banana · umbrella · bed

ribbon · guitar · raccoon · rattle

feather · foot · fan · egg

hat · goat · hammer · ham

Beginning Sounds

Name_____

Name the pictures. In each row, circle the pictures that begin with the same sound as the first picture in the row.

wagon · van · window · worm

zero · zipper · pot · zebra

nail · nest · nine · kite

queen · quilt · rope · quarter

Ending Sounds

Name_____

Name the pictures. In each row, circle the pictures that end with the same sound as the first picture in the row.

dog · egg · pig · leaf

bell · pool · drum · seal

star · mop · guitar · jar

hive · five · web · glove

Ending Sounds

Name_____

Name the pictures. In each row, circle the pictures that end with the same sound as the first picture in the row.

bus · dress · frog · grass

hook · boot · beak · book

mop · sheep · cup · mailbox

cat · coat · top · peanut

Consonants: *S*

Name _____

The sound at the beginning of **sun** is spelled by the letter **s**.

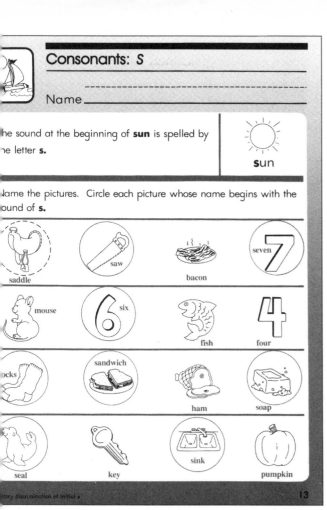

sun

Name the pictures. Circle each picture whose name begins with the sound of **s**.

saddle · saw · bacon · seven 7 · mouse · six 6 · fish · four 4 · socks · sandwich · ham · soap · seal · key · sink · pumpkin

---

Consonants: *S*

Name _____

Name the pictures. Write **s** below each picture whose name begins with the sound of **s**.

sun

salad · kite · sink S

five 5 · six 6 · S · soap S

saw · seal S · horse

S · S

Consonants: *S*

Name _____

Name the pictures. Draw a line from the letter **s** to the picture whose name begins with the sound of **s**.

sun

soup · deer · seven 7 · bike · suit · goat · towel · sandwich · ten 10 · six 6 · soap · can · seal · pot · rake · socks

---

Consonants: *M*

Name _____

The sound at the beginning of **mouse** is spelled by the letter **m**.

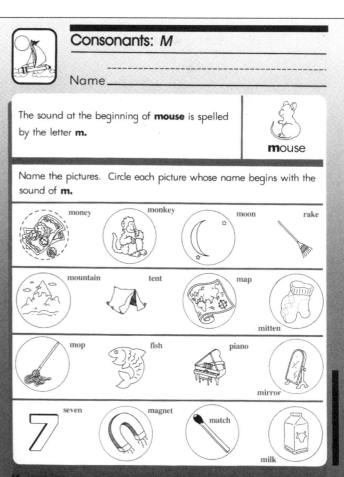

mouse

Name the pictures. Circle each picture whose name begins with the sound of **m**.

money · monkey · moon · rake · mountain · tent · map · mitten · mop · fish · piano · mirror · seven 7 · magnet · match · milk

Consonants: M

Name_____

Name the pictures. Write **m** below each picture whose name begins with the sound of **m.**

mouse

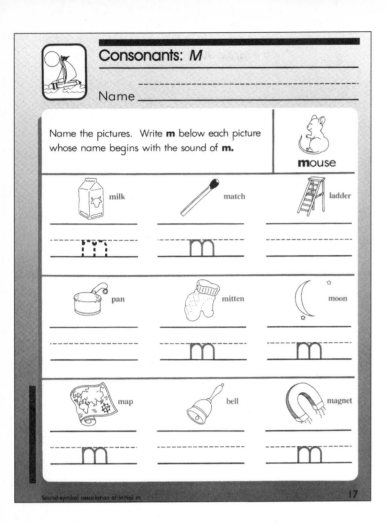

milk	match	ladder
mm	m	
pan	mitten	moon
	m	m
map	bell	magnet
m		m

Consonants: M

Name_____

Name the pictures. Draw a line from each letter to the picture whose name begins with that letter.

mouse

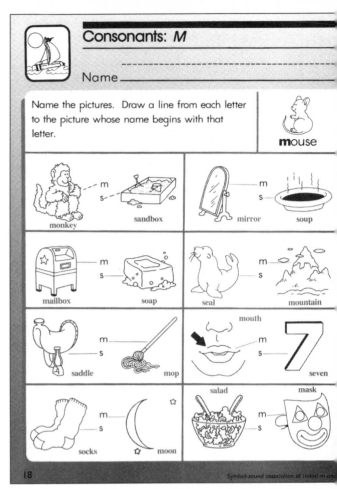

monkey — m / sandbox — s
mirror — m / soup — s
mailbox — m / soap — s
seal — m / mountain — s
saddle — m / mop — s
mouth — m / seven — s
socks — m / moon — s
salad — m / mask — s

Consonants: T

Name_____

The sound at the beginning of **tent** is spelled by the letter **t.**

tent

Name the pictures. Circle each picture whose name begins with the sound of **t.**

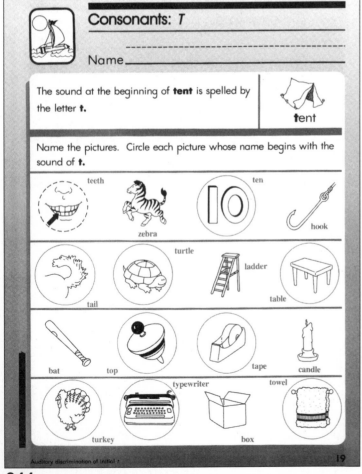

teeth • zebra • ten • hook
tail • turtle • ladder • table
bat • top • tape • candle
turkey • typewriter • box • towel

Consonants: T

Name_____

Name the pictures. Write **t** below each picture whose name begins with the sound of **t.**

tent

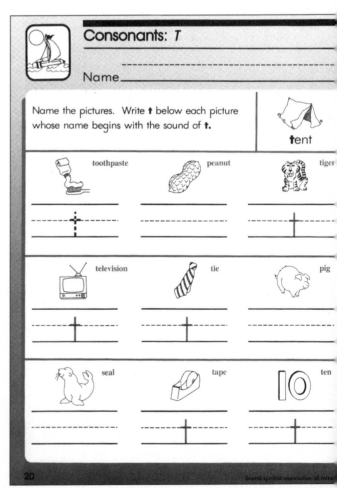

toothpaste	peanut	tiger
t		t
television	tie	pig
t	t	
seal	tape	ten
	t	t

Name the pictures. Draw a line from each letter to the picture whose name begins with that letter.

tent

Symbol-sound association of initial *t* and other consonants

21

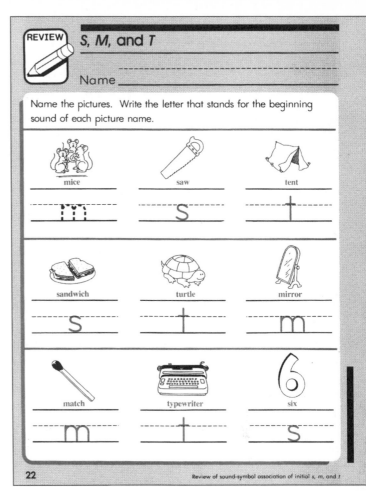

Name the pictures. Write the letter that stands for the beginning sound of each picture name.

22

Review of sound-symbol association of initial *s, m,* and *t*

Ending Sounds: S, M, and T

Name

The sound at the end of **bus** is spelled by the letter **s**.
The sound at the end of **ham** is spelled by the letter **m**.
The sound at the end of **cat** is spelled by the letter **t**.

bu**s**
ha**m**
ca**t**

Look at the pictures. Circle the letter that stands for the sound you hear at the end of the picture name.

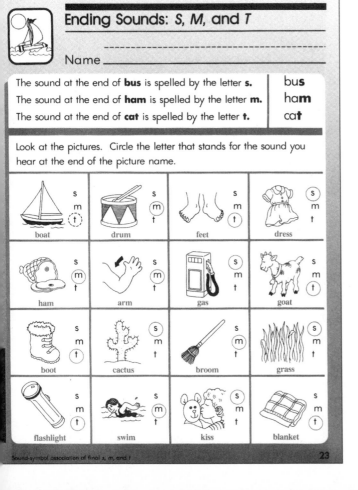

Sound-symbol association of final *s, m,* and *t*

23

Consonants: P

Name

The sound at the beginning of **pig** is spelled by the letter **p**.

pig

Name the pictures. Circle each picture whose name begins with the sound of **p**.

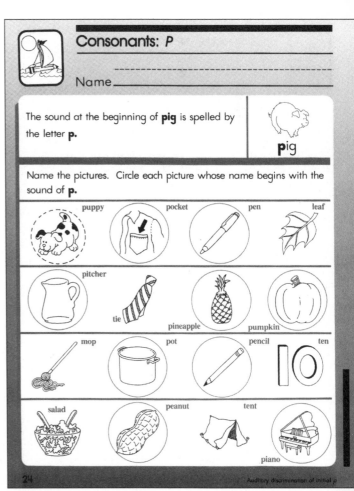

24

Auditory discrimination of initial *p*

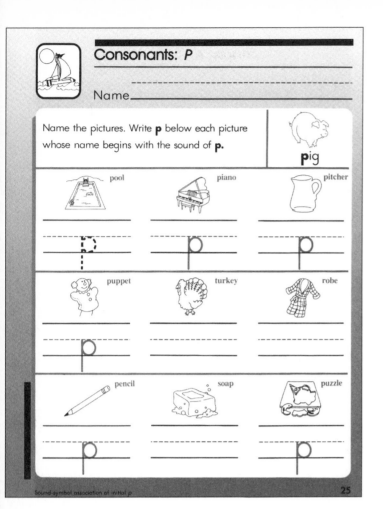

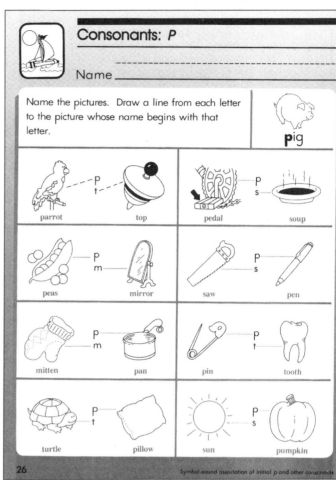

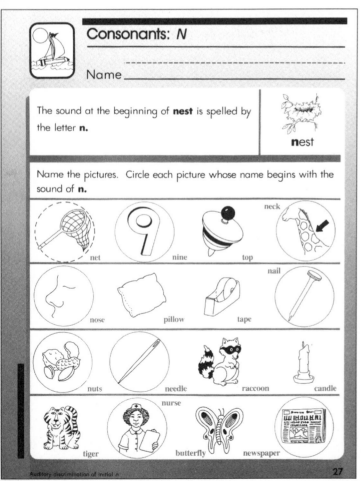

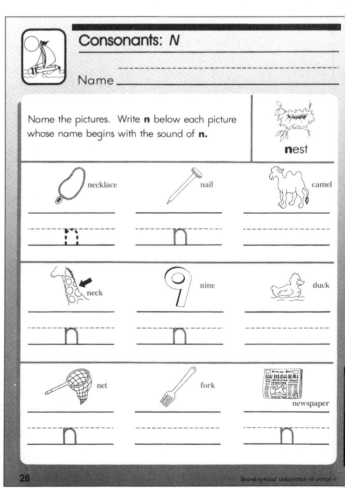

Consonants: N

Name

Name the pictures. Draw a line from each letter to the picture whose name begins with that letter.

nest

ten — nine — seal — needle

match — nail — nuts — piano

nurse — socks — nose — telephone

pencil — net — newspaper — mitten

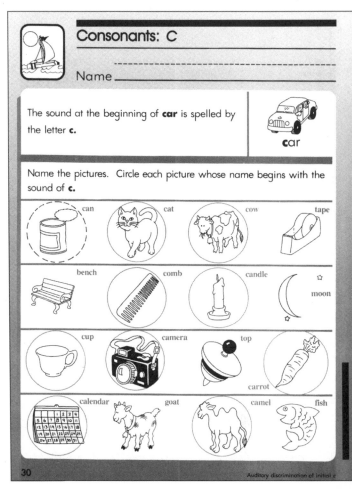

Consonants: C

Name

The sound at the beginning of **car** is spelled by the letter **c**.

car

Name the pictures. Circle each picture whose name begins with the sound of **c**.

can — cat — cow — tape

bench — comb — candle — moon

cup — camera — top — carrot

calendar — goat — camel — fish

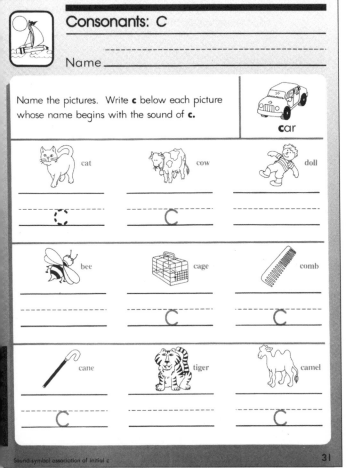

Consonants: C

Name

Name the pictures. Write **c** below each picture whose name begins with the sound of **c**.

car

cat — cow — doll

bee — cage — comb

cane — tiger — camel

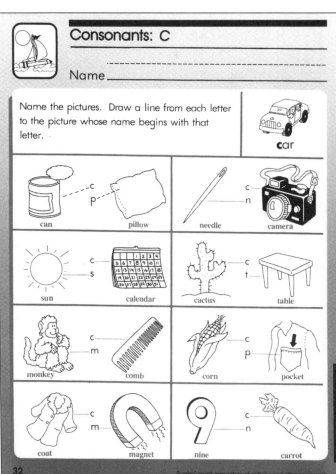

Consonants: C

Name

Name the pictures. Draw a line from each letter to the picture whose name begins with that letter.

car

can — pillow — needle — camera

sun — calendar — cactus — table

monkey — comb — corn — pocket

coat — magnet — nine — carrot

P, N, and C

Name_____

Name the pictures. Write the letter that stands for the beginning sound of each picture name.

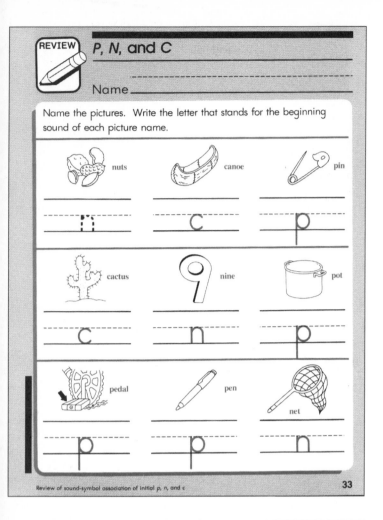

nuts — **n**

canoe — **c**

pin — **p**

cactus — **c**

nine — **n**

pot — **p**

pedal — **p**

pen — **p**

net — **n**

Ending Sounds: P, N, and C

Name_____

The sound at the end of **moon** is spelled by the letter **n.** The sound at the end of **mop** is spelled by the letter **p.** The sound at the end of **magic** is spelled by the letter **c.**

moo**n**
mo**p**
magi**c**

Name the pictures. Circle the letter that stands for the sound you hear at the end of each picture name.

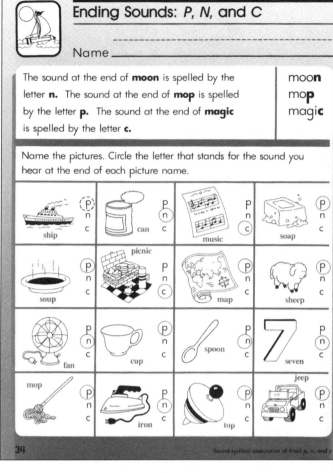

Consonants: K

Name_____

The sound at the beginning of **kitten** is spelled by the letter **k.**

kitten

Name the pictures. Circle each picture whose name begins with the sound of **k.**

Consonants: K

Name_____

Name the pictures. Write **k** below each picture whose name begins with the sound of **k.**

kitten

248

Name

Look at the pictures. Draw a line from each letter to the picture whose name begins with that letter.

kitten

key k p parrot

king tail

k t

tape k t kitten

kitchen k p pencil

kite k n nail

saw k s kangaroo

kite mountain k m

nine kiss k n

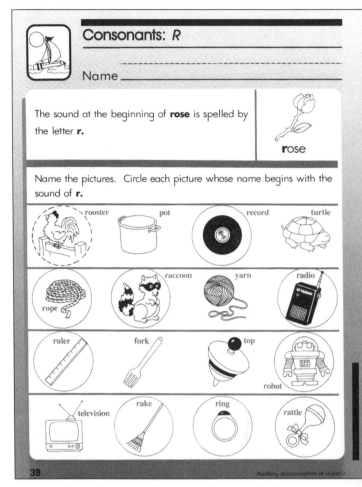

Name

The sound at the beginning of **rose** is spelled by the letter **r.**

rose

Name the pictures. Circle each picture whose name begins with the sound of **r.**

rooster — pot — record — turtle

rope — raccoon — yarn — radio

ruler — fork — top — robot

television — rake — ring — rattle

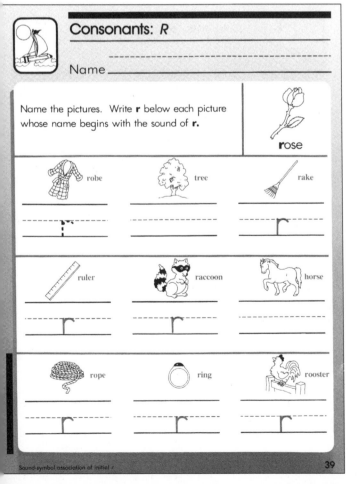

Name

Name the pictures. Write **r** below each picture whose name begins with the sound of **r.**

rose

robe — tree — rake

ruler — raccoon — horse

rope — ring — rooster

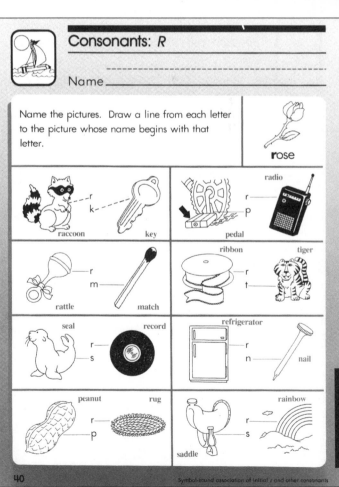

Name

Name the pictures. Draw a line from each letter to the picture whose name begins with that letter.

rose

raccoon r k key

pedal r p radio

rattle r m match

ribbon r t tiger

seal r s record

refrigerator r n nail

peanut rug r p

saddle r s rainbow

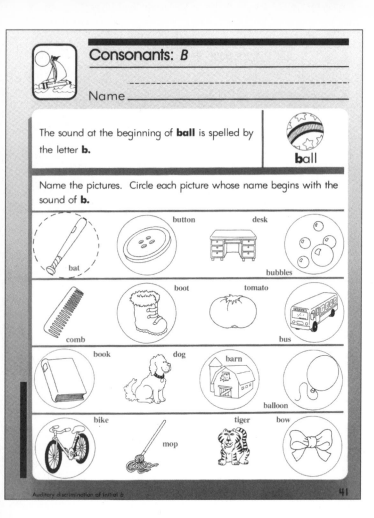

Consonants: B

Name _____

The sound at the beginning of **ball** is spelled by the letter **b**.

ball

Name the pictures. Circle each picture whose name begins with the sound of **b**.

bat · button · desk · bubbles

comb · boot · tomato · bus

book · dog · barn · balloon

bike · mop · tiger · bow

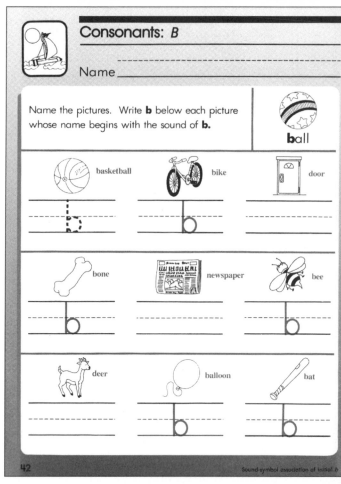

Consonants: B

Name _____

Name the pictures. Write **b** below each picture whose name begins with the sound of **b**.

ball

basketball   bike   door

bone   newspaper   bee

deer   balloon   bat

Consonants: B

Name _____

Name the pictures. Draw a line from each letter to the picture whose name begins with that letter.

ball

basketball · rain — b, r

can · bell — b, c

soap · bed — b, s

book · monkey — b, m

box · kitten — b, k

button · robot — b, r

needle · banana — b, n

typewriter · butterfly — b, t

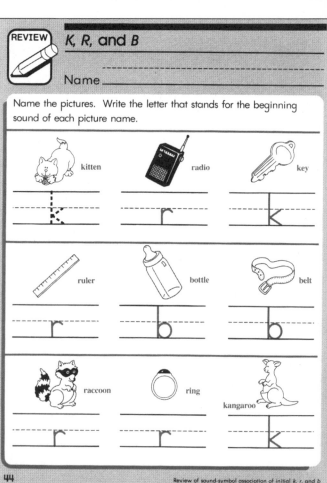

REVIEW

K, R, and B

Name _____

Name the pictures. Write the letter that stands for the beginning sound of each picture name.

kitten   radio   key

ruler   bottle   belt

raccoon   ring   kangaroo

Ending Sounds: K, R, and B

Name

The sound at the end of **book** is spelled by the letter **k**. The sound at the end of **four** is spelled by the letter **r**. The sound at the end of **tub** is spelled by the letter **b**.

boo**k**
fou**r**
tu**b**

Name the pictures. Circle the letter that stands for the sound you hear at the end of each picture name.

crib — k r (b)
door — k r b
star — k r b
bib — k r (b)

deer — k (r) b
bathtub — k r (b)
tiger — k (r) b
doorknob — k r (b)

hook — (k) r b
crab — k r (b)
web — k r (b)
book — (k) r b

mirror — k (r) b
guitar — k (r) b
beak — (k) r b
car — k (r) b

Sound-symbol association of final k, r, and b

45

Consonants: J

Name

The sound at the beginning of **jet** is spelled by the letter **j**.

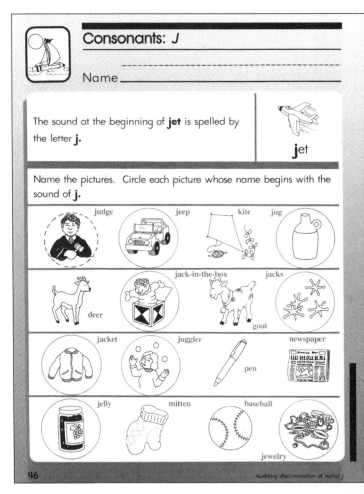

jet

Name the pictures. Circle each picture whose name begins with the sound of **j**.

judge · jeep · kite · jug

deer · jack-in-the-box · jacks · goat

jacket · juggler · pen · newspaper

jelly · mitten · baseball · jewelry

46

Auditory discrimination of initial j

Consonants: J

Name

Name the pictures. Write **j** below each picture whose name begins with the sound of **j**.

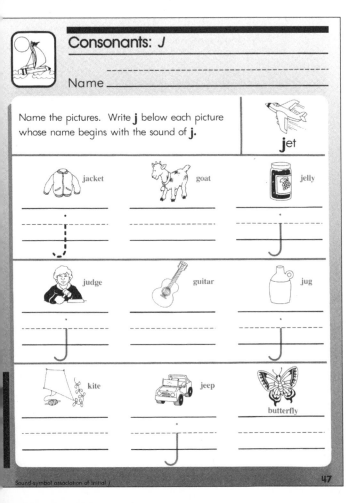

jet

jacket · goat · jelly

judge · guitar · jug

kite · jeep · butterfly

Sound-symbol association of initial j

47

Consonants: J

Name

Name the pictures. Draw a line from each letter to the picture whose name begins with that letter.

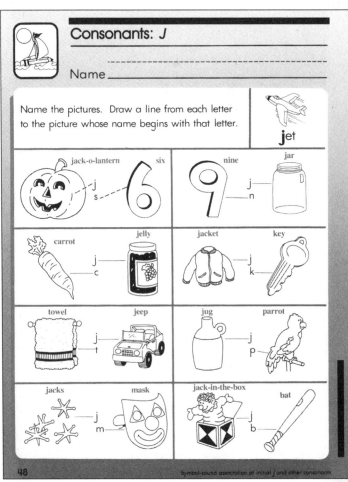

jet

jack-o-lantern — j/s — six · nine · jar — j/n

carrot — j/c · jelly · jacket — j/k · key

towel — j/t · jeep · jug — j/p · parrot

jacks — j/m · mask · jack-in-the-box — j/b · bat

48

Symbol-sound association of initial j and other consonants

251

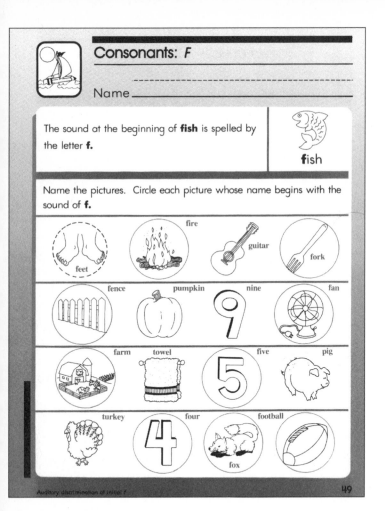

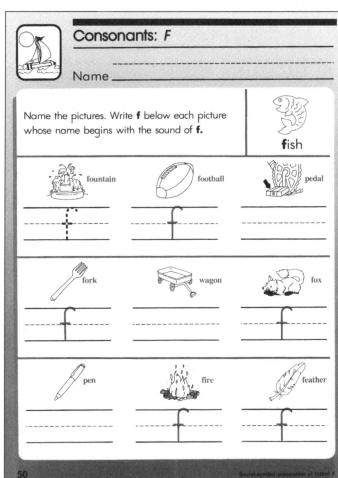

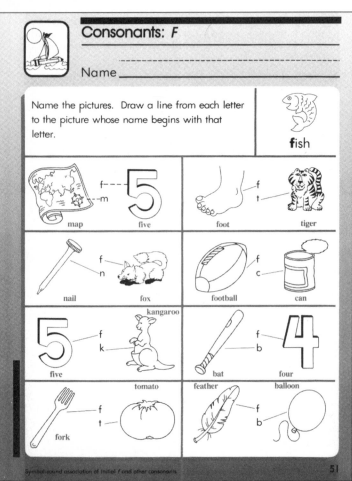

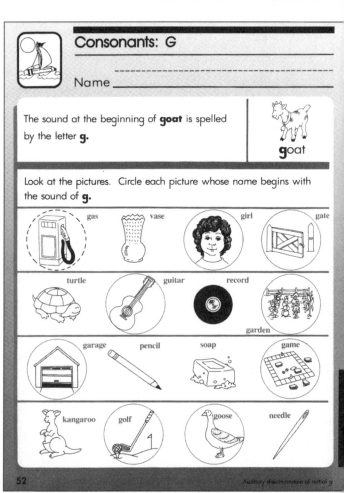

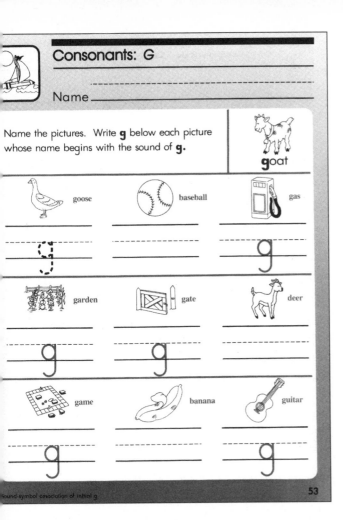

Consonants: G

Name_____

Name the pictures. Write **g** below each picture whose name begins with the sound of **g.**

goat

goose	baseball	gas
g		g
garden	gate	deer
g	g	
game	banana	guitar
g		g

Consonants: G

Name_____

Look at the pictures. Draw a line from each letter to the picture whose name begins with that letter.

goat

golf feather	pencil girl
g f	g p
telephone garden	gate pineapple
g t	g p
moon garage	seal goose
g m	g s
guitar bee	refrigerator game
g b	g r

Sound-symbol association of initial g.   53

54   Symbol-sound association of initial g and other consonants

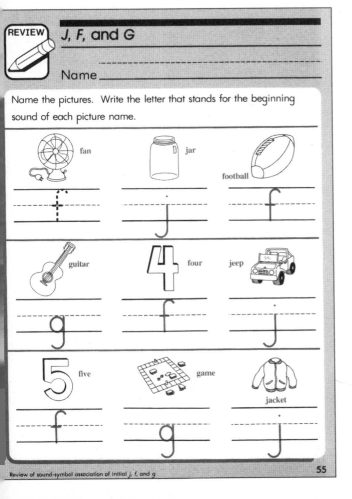

J, F, and G

Name_____

Name the pictures. Write the letter that stands for the beginning sound of each picture name.

fan	jar	football
f	j	f
guitar	four	jeep
g	f	j
five	game	jacket
f	g	j

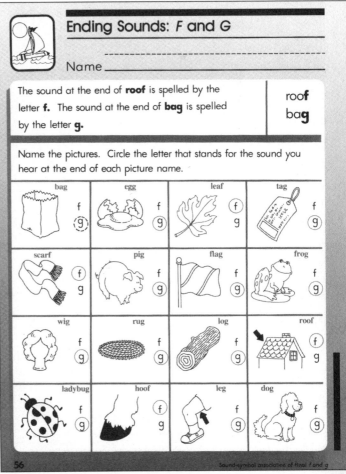

Ending Sounds: F and G

Name_____

The sound at the end of **roof** is spelled by the letter **f.** The sound at the end of **bag** is spelled by the letter **g.**

roo**f**
ba**g**

Name the pictures. Circle the letter that stands for the sound you hear at the end of each picture name.

bag	egg	leaf	tag
f (g)	f (g)	(f) g	f (g)
scarf	pig	flag	frog
(f) g	f (g)	f (g)	f (g)
wig	rug	log	roof
f (g)	f (g)	f (g)	(f) g
ladybug	hoof	leg	dog
f (g)	(f) g	f (g)	f (g)

Review of sound-symbol association of initial j, f, and g.   55

56   Sound-symbol associations of final f and g

253

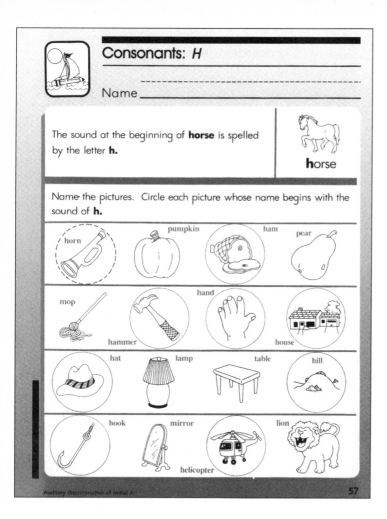

Consonants: H

Name _____

The sound at the beginning of **horse** is spelled by the letter **h.**

horse

Name the pictures. Circle each picture whose name begins with the sound of **h.**

horn pumpkin ham pear

mop hammer hand house

hat lamp table hill

hook mirror helicopter lion

Consonants: H

Name _____

Name the pictures. Write **h** below each picture whose name begins with the sound of **h.**

horse

house hat desk

hook guitar hammer

hamburger kite helicopter

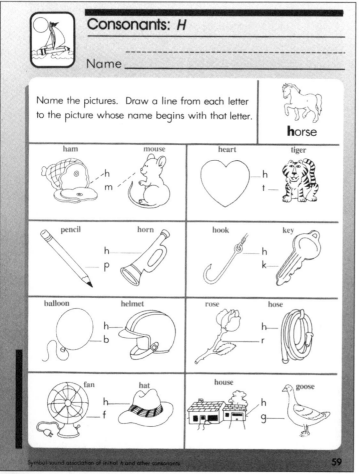

Consonants: H

Name _____

Name the pictures. Draw a line from each letter to the picture whose name begins with that letter.

horse

ham mouse
h
m

heart tiger
h
t

pencil horn
h
p

hook key
h
k

balloon helmet
h
b

rose hose
h
r

fan hat
h
f

house goose
h
g

Consonants: D

Name _____

The sound at the beginning of **dog** is spelled by the letter **d.**

dog

Look at the pictures. Circle each picture whose name begins with the sound of **d.**

duck bee doctor doll

deer dive heart kite

desk mouse dishes belt

feather door dominoes dinosaur

254

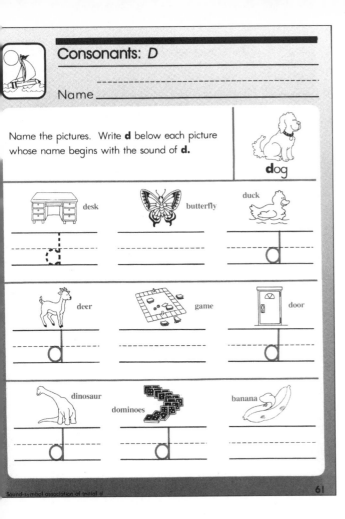

Consonants: D

Name _____

dog

Name the pictures. Write **d** below each picture whose name begins with the sound of **d.**

desk   butterfly   duck

deer   game   door

dinosaur   dominoes   banana

Consonants: D

Name _____

dog

Name the pictures. Draw a line from each letter to the picture whose name begins with that letter.

pot   dock   desk   can
d   p   d   c

doll   feather   turtle   dinosaur
d   f   d   t

doctor   ring   duck   belt
d   r   d   b

tomato   deer   door   goat
d   t   d   g

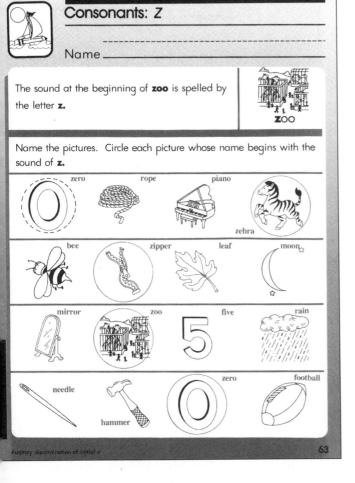

Consonants: Z

Name _____

zoo

The sound at the beginning of **zoo** is spelled by the letter **z.**

Name the pictures. Circle each picture whose name begins with the sound of **z.**

zero   rope   piano   zebra

bee   zipper   leaf   moon

mirror   zoo   five   rain

needle   hammer   zero   football

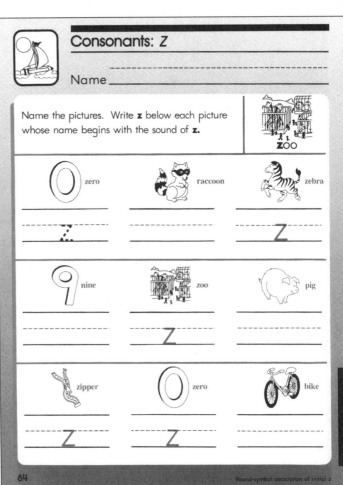

Consonants: Z

Name _____

zoo

Name the pictures. Write **z** below each picture whose name begins with the sound of **z.**

zero   raccoon   zebra

nine   zoo   pig

zipper   zero   bike

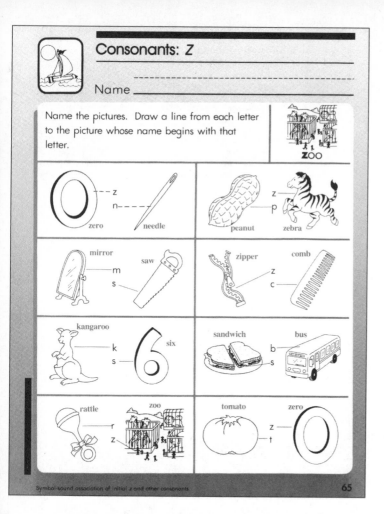

Consonants: Z

Name _____

Name the pictures. Draw a line from each letter to the picture whose name begins with that letter.

zoo

zero — z
needle — n

peanut — zebra
z
p

mirror — m
saw — s

zipper — z
comb — c

kangaroo — k
six — s

sandwich — b
bus — s

rattle — r
zoo — z

tomato — z
zero — t

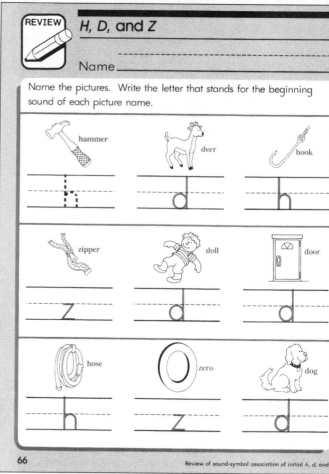

REVIEW H, D, and Z

Name _____

Name the pictures. Write the letter that stands for the beginning sound of each picture name.

hammer — h

deer — d

hook — h

zipper — z

doll — d

door — o

hose — h

zero — z

dog — d

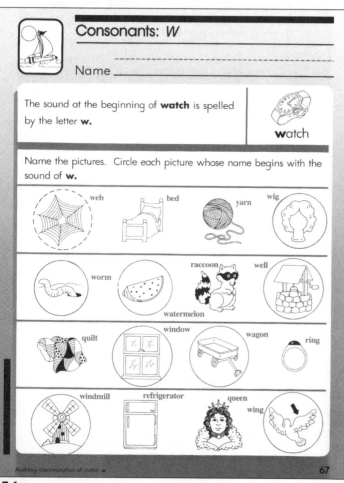

Consonants: W

Name _____

The sound at the beginning of **watch** is spelled by the letter **w.**

watch

Name the pictures. Circle each picture whose name begins with the sound of **w.**

web   bed   yarn   wig

worm   watermelon   raccoon   well

quilt   window   wagon   ring

windmill   refrigerator   queen   wing

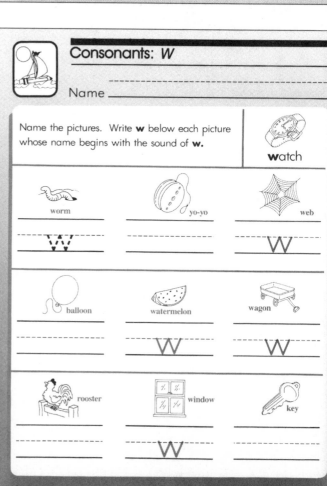

Consonants: W

Name _____

Name the pictures. Write **w** below each picture whose name begins with the sound of **w.**

watch

worm   yo-yo   web
W   W

balloon   watermelon   wagon
                W   W

rooster   window   key

W

Consonants: W

Name _____

Name the pictures. Draw a line from each letter to the picture whose name begins with that letter.

watch

windmill — w
cat — c

dominoes — d
wig — w

zebra — w
worm — z

watermelon — w
button — b

piano — w
window — p

milk — w
well — m

wing — w
jar — j

wagon — w
guitar — g

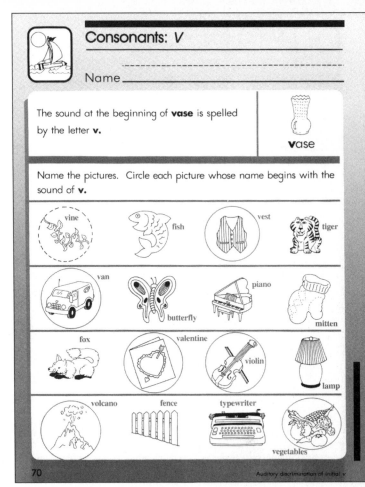

Consonants: V

Name _____

The sound at the beginning of **vase** is spelled by the letter **v.**

vase

Name the pictures. Circle each picture whose name begins with the sound of **v.**

vine   fish   vest   tiger

van   butterfly   piano   mitten

fox   valentine   violin   lamp

volcano   fence   typewriter   vegetables

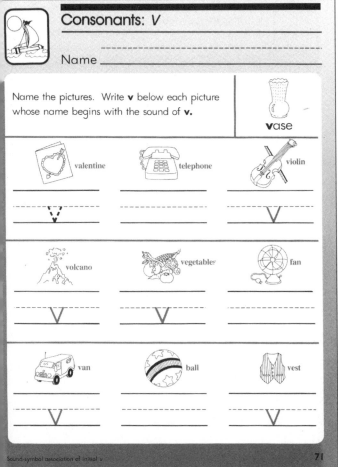

Consonants: V

Name _____

Name the pictures. Write **v** below each picture whose name begins with the sound of **v.**

vase

valentine   telephone   violin

volcano   vegetables   fan

van   ball   vest

Consonants: V

Name _____

Name the pictures. Draw a line from each letter to the picture whose name begins with that letter.

vase

tent — t
vine — v

radio — r
violin — v

van — v
feather — f

vest — v
zebra — z

carrot — c
vase — v

vegetables — v
moon — m

wagon — w
valentine — v

gate — g
volcano — v

Consonants: L

Name _____

The sound at the beginning of **lion** is spelled by the letter **l**.

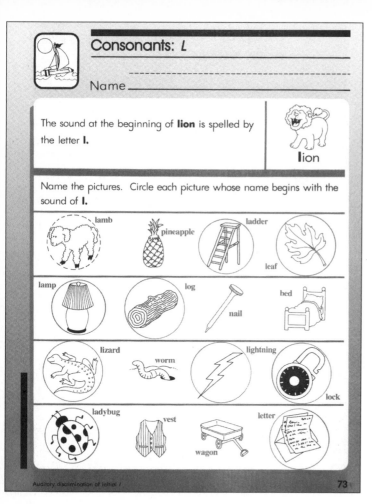

lion

Name the pictures. Circle each picture whose name begins with the sound of **l**.

lamb
pineapple
ladder
leaf

lamp
log
nail
bed

lizard
worm
lightning
lock

ladybug
vest
wagon
letter

Consonants: L

Name _____

Name the pictures. Write **l** below each picture whose name begins with the sound of **l**.

lion

letter
ladder
banana

leaves
log
window

lightning
ruler
lizard

Consonants: L

Name _____

Name the pictures. Draw a line from each letter to the picture whose name begins with that letter.

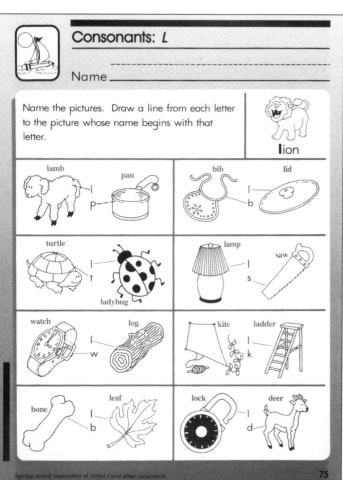

lion

lamb   pan

bib   lid
l
b

turtle
l
t
ladybug

lamp
l
s
saw

watch
l
w
log

kite
l
k
ladder

bone
l
b
leaf

lock
l
d
deer

W, V, and L

Name _____

Name the pictures. Write the letter that stands for the beginning sound of each picture name.

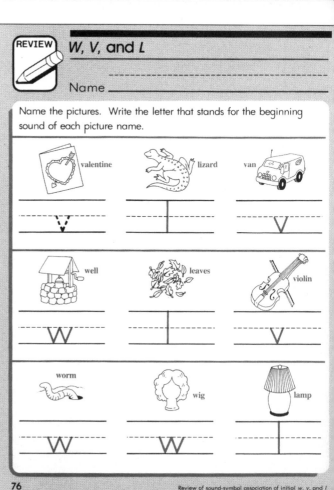

valentine
lizard
van
V

well
leaves
violin
W
V

worm
wig
lamp
W
W

258

Ending Sounds: D and L

Name _____

The sound at the end of **road** is spelled by the letter **d**. The sound at the end of **girl** is spelled by the letter **l**.

roa**d**
gir**l**

Name the pictures. Circle the letter that stands for the sound you hear at the end of each picture name.

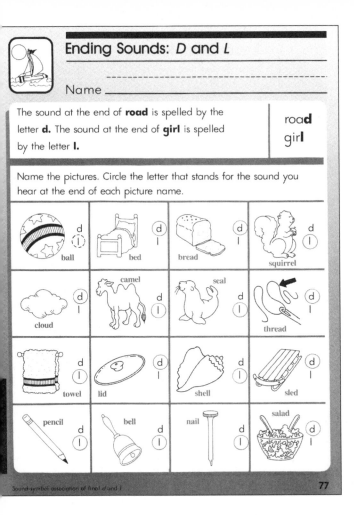

ball — **d** l	bed — d l	bread — d l	squirrel — d l
cloud — d l	camel — d l	seal — d l	thread — d l
towel — d l	lid — d l	shell — d l	sled — d l
pencil — d l	bell — d l	nail — d l	salad — d l

Consonants: Y

Name _____

The sound at the beginning of **yard** is spelled by the letter **y**.

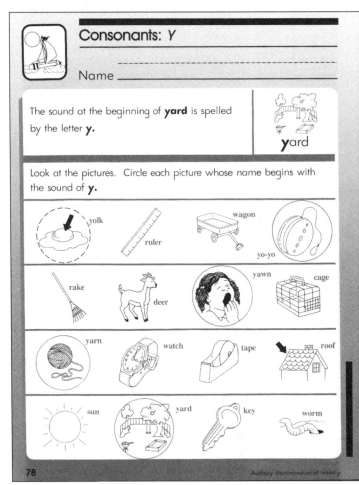

yard

Look at the pictures. Circle each picture whose name begins with the sound of **y**.

yolk	ruler	wagon	yo-yo
rake	deer	yawn	cage
yarn	watch	tape	roof
sun	yard	key	worm

Consonants: Y

Name _____

Look at the pictures. Write **y** below each picture whose name begins with the sound of **y**.

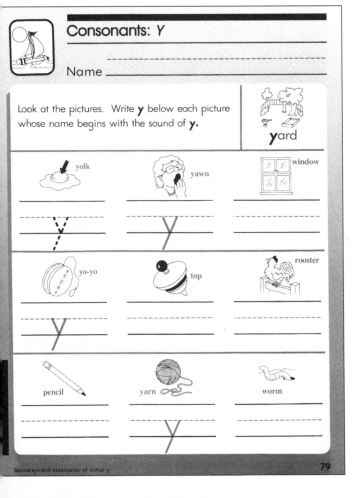

yard

yolk	yawn	window
yo-yo	top	rooster
pencil	yarn	worm

Consonants: Y

Name _____

Look at the pictures. Draw a line from each letter to the picture whose name begins with that letter.

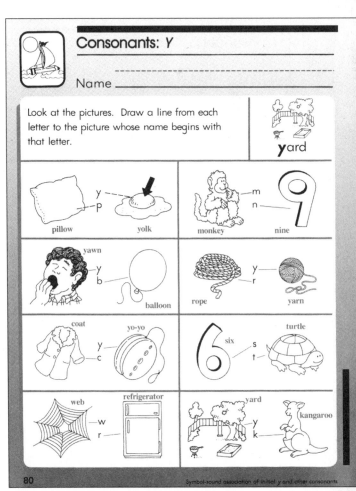

yard

pillow y / p yolk	monkey m / n nine
yawn y / b balloon	rope y / r yarn
coat y / c yo-yo	six s / t turtle
web w / r refrigerator	yard y / k kangaroo

Consonants: X

Name _____

The sound at the end of **ax** is spelled by the letter **x**.

a**x**

Name the pictures. Circle each picture whose name ends with the sound of **x**.

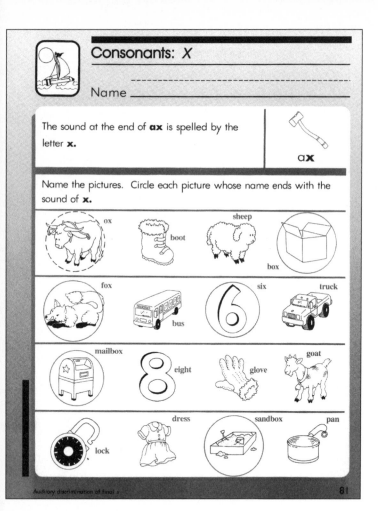

ox · boot · sheep · box

fox · bus · six · truck

mailbox · eight · glove · goat

lock · dress · sandbox · pan

Consonants: X

Name _____

Name the pictures. Write **x** below each picture whose name ends with the sound of **x**.

a**x**

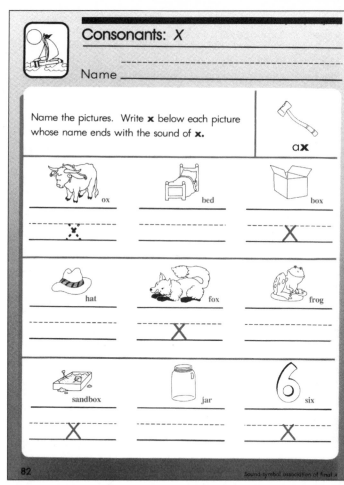

ox · bed · box

hat · fox · frog

sandbox · jar · six

Consonants: X

Name _____

Name the pictures. Draw a line from each letter to the picture whose name ends with that letter.

a**x**

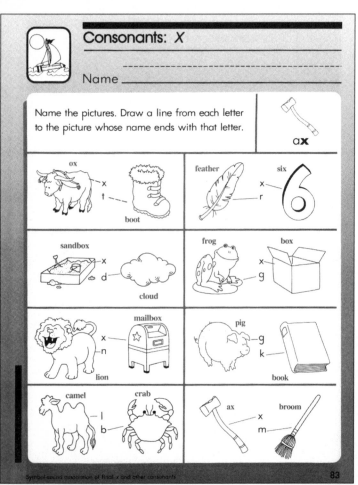

ox · x · t · boot

feather · six · x · r

sandbox · x · d · cloud

frog · box · x · g

lion · mailbox · x · n

pig · g · k · book

camel · crab · l · b

ax · x · m · broom

Consonants: Qu

Name _____

The sound at the beginning of **quilt** is spelled by the letters **qu**.

quilt

Look at the pictures. Circle each picture whose name begins with the sound of **qu**.

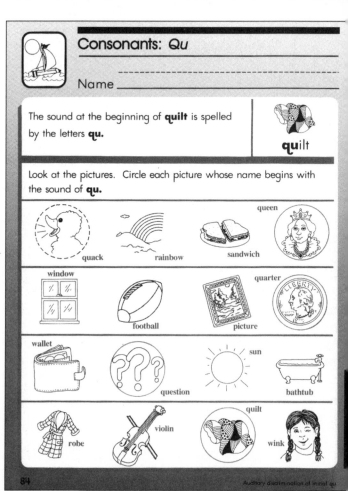

quack · rainbow · sandwich · queen

window · football · picture · quarter

wallet · question · sun · bathtub

robe · violin · quilt · wink

Consonants: *Qu*

Name

Look at the pictures. Write **qu** below each picture whose name begins with the sound of **qu**.

quilt

queen   quack   wagon

qu   qu

quarter   bed   deer

qu

quilt   butterfly   question

qu   qu

Consonants: *Qu*

Name

Look at the pictures. Draw a line from each letter or pair of letters to the picture whose name begins with that letter or pair of letters.

quilt

quack   qu / z   zebra
car   c / g   goat
soap   s / k   key
wing   qu / w   queen
quilt   qu / v   violin
jeep   f / j   feather
question   qu / b   bus
pitcher   qu / p   quarter

REVIEW — *Y* and *Qu*

Name

Look at the pictures. Write the letter or pair of letters that stands for the beginning sound of each picture name.

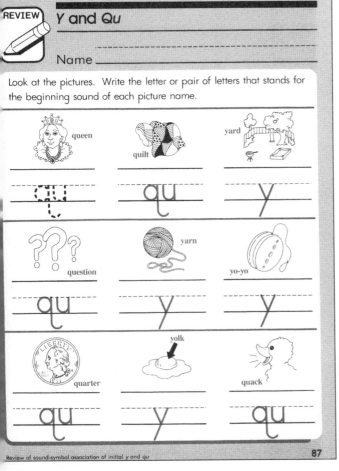

queen   quilt   yard

qu   qu   y

question   yarn   yo-yo

qu   y   y

quarter   yolk   quack

qu   y   qu

REVIEW — Ending Sounds

Parent Involvement Master 1, Page T-41

Name

Name the pictures. Write the letter that stands for the ending sound of each picture name.

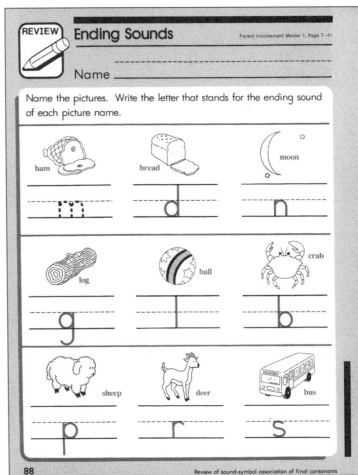

ham   bread   moon

m   d   n

log   ball   crab

g   l   b

sheep   deer   bus

p   r   s

Consonants

Name _____

Name the pictures. Write the letters that stand for the beginning and ending sounds of each picture name.

dog   nut   mop

fox   bat   sun

ham   lid   rug

Assessment of sound-symbol association of initial and final consonants   89

Short A

Name _____

Fan has the short-**a** sound. This sound is usually spelled by the letter **a**.

fan

Name the pictures. Circle each picture whose name has the short-**a** sound.

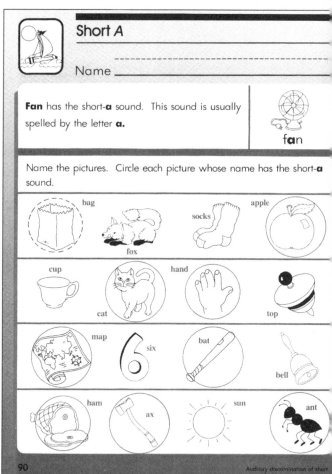

bag   fox   socks   apple

cup   cat   hand   top

map   six   bat   bell

ham   ax   sun   ant

90   Auditory discrimination of short

Short A

Name _____

Name the pictures. Write **a** below each picture whose name has the short-**a** sound.

fan

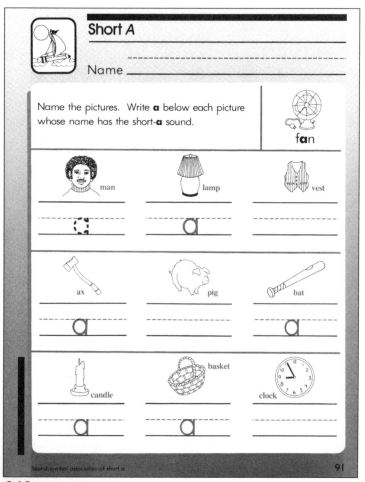

man   lamp   vest

a   a

ax   pig   bat

a   a

candle   basket   clock

a   a

Sound-symbol association of short a   91

Short A

Name _____

Read the words and name the pictures. Draw a line from each word to the picture it names.

fan

bag / bat   cap / cat

hat / ham   map / mat

tag / ax   van / man

pan / fan   can / cab

92   Symbol-sound association of short-a words

262

Short A

Name _____

Read each sentence and the words beside it. Write the word that makes sense in each sentence.

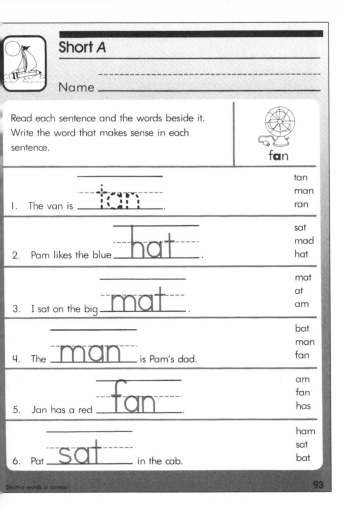

fan

1. The van is __**tan**__ .

tan
man
ran

2. Pam likes the blue __**hat**__ .

sat
mad
hat

3. I sat on the big __**mat**__ .

mat
at
am

4. The __**man**__ is Pam's dad.

bat
man
fan

5. Jan has a red __**fan**__ .

am
fan
has

6. Pat __**sat**__ in the cab.

ham
sat
bat

Short-a words in context   93

Short I

Name _____

Bib has the short-**i** sound. This sound is usually spelled by the letter **i**.

bib

Name the pictures. Circle each picture whose name has the short-**i** sound.

hill · hat · pig · brick

crib · pot · bat · dishes

drum · six · milk · tent

quilt · belt · fish · box

94   Auditory discrimination of short i

Short I

Name _____

Name the pictures. Write **i** below each picture whose name has the short-**i** sound.

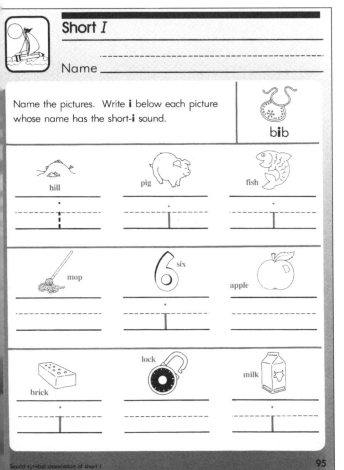

bib

hill · pig · fish

mop · six · apple

brick · lock · milk

Sound-symbol association of short i   95

Short I

Name _____

Read the words and look at the pictures. Draw a line from each word to the picture it tells about.

bib

six
sit

pig
dig

mitt
mix

hit
hill

wig
win

zip
rip

dig
wig

lid
lips

96   Symbol-sound association of short-i words

263

Short I

Name _____

Read each sentence and the words beside it. Write the word that makes sense in each sentence.

bib

			fit wig did
1.	Will this hat	Tim?	

| 2. | Jan will _____ the car with gas. | wig
his
fill |

| 3. | Jim said his cat was _____. | ill
is
if |

| 4. | The pig _____ on the hill. | six
kid
hid |

| 5. | Jill _____ the ball with the bat. | hit
his
pin |

| 6. | Is the _____ on the pan? | hills
lid
him |

REVIEW Short A and I

Name _____

Read the words and look at the pictures. Circle the word that tells about each picture.

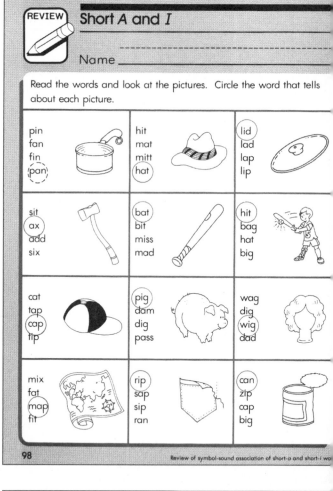

pin fan fin (pan)	hit mat mitt (hat)	(lid) lad lap lip
sit (ax) add six	(bat) bit miss mad	hit (bag) hat big
cat tap (cap) tip	(pig) dam dig pass	wag dig (wig) dad
mix fat (map) fit	(rip) sap sip ran	(can) zip cap big

Short O

Name _____

Top has the short-**o** sound. This sound is usually spelled by the letter **o**.

t**o**p

Name the pictures. Circle each picture whose name has the short-**o** sound.

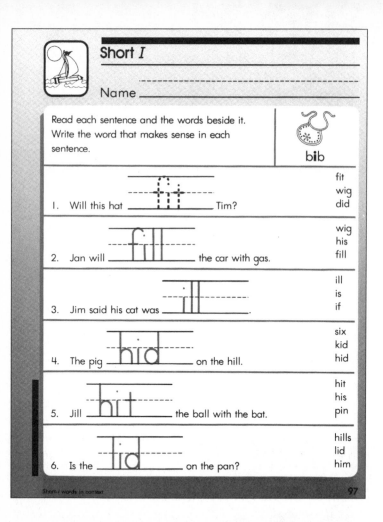

doll   box   bat   block

clock   cup   fox   bell

bottle   pot   rocket   tent

ham   sock   bib   mop

Short O

Name _____

Name the pictures. Write **o** below each picture whose name has the short-**o** sound.

t**o**p

block   fox   cat

cup   ten   clock

mop   lock   ant

Read the words and look at the pictures. Draw a line from each word to the picture it tells about.

t**o**p

box
fax

doll
dots

cob
cot

hot
hop

pop
pot

mop
rod

ox
top

hog
log

Read each sentence and the words beside it. Write the word that makes sense in each sentence.

t**o**p

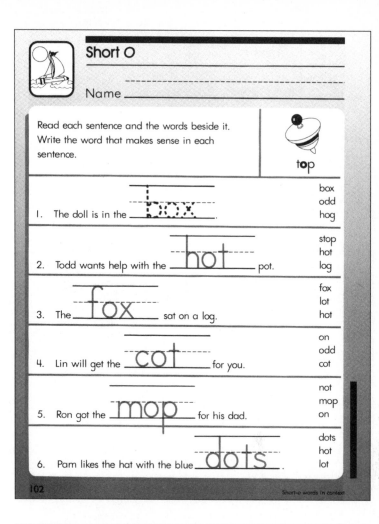

1. The doll is in the ___box___ .

box
odd
hog

2. Todd wants help with the ___hot___ pot.

stop
hot
log

3. The ___fox___ sat on a log.

fox
lot
hot

4. Lin will get the ___cot___ for you.

on
odd
cot

5. Ron got the ___mop___ for his dad.

not
mop
on

6. Pam likes the hat with the blue ___dots___ .

dots
hot
lot

Bed has the short-**e** sound. This sound is usually spelled by the letter **e.**

b**e**d

Name the pictures. Circle each picture whose name has the short-**e** sound.

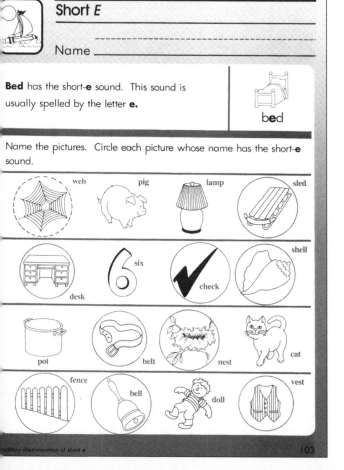

web   pig   lamp   sled

desk   six   check   shell

pot   belt   nest   cat

fence   bell   doll   vest

Name the pictures. Write **e** below each picture whose name has the short-**e** sound.

b**e**d

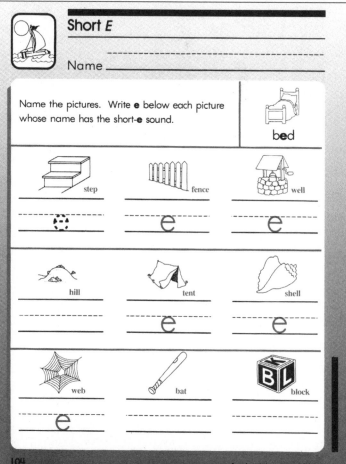

step   fence   well
___   e   e

hill   tent   shell
        e   e

web   bat   block
e

Short E

Name _____

Read the words and look at the pictures. Draw a line from each word to the picture it tells about.

b**e**d

leg
ten

wet
jet

bell
well

pet
net

wet
web

egg
fell

men
hen

beg
bed

Short E

Name _____

Read each sentence and the words beside it. Write the word that makes sense in each sentence.

b**e**d

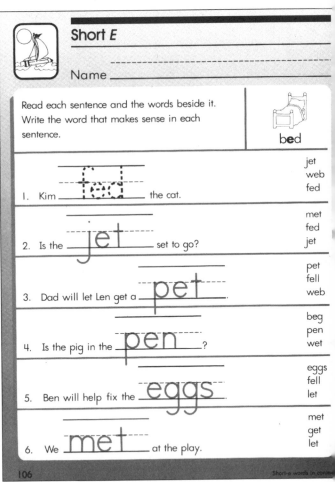

1. Kim _____ the cat.
   - jet
   - web
   - fed

2. Is the _jet_ set to go?
   - met
   - fed
   - jet

3. Dad will let Len get a _pet_.
   - pet
   - fell
   - web

4. Is the pig in the _pen_?
   - beg
   - pen
   - wet

5. Ben will help fix the _eggs_.
   - eggs
   - fell
   - let

6. We _met_ at the play.
   - met
   - get
   - let

Short O and E

Name _____

Read the words and look at the pictures. Circle the word that tells about each picture.

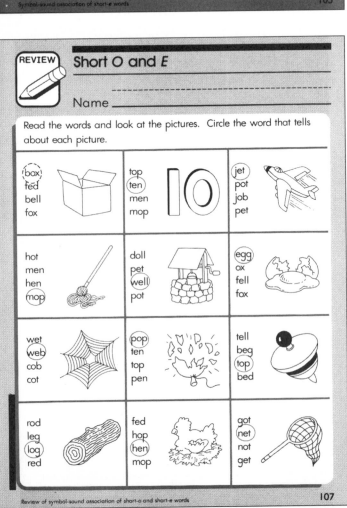

box
fed
bell
fox

top
ten
men
mop

jet
pot
job
pet

hot
men
hen
mop

doll
pet
well
pot

egg
ox
fell
fox

wet
web
cob
cot

pop
ten
top
pen

tell
beg
top
bed

rod
leg
log
red

fed
hop
hen
mop

got
net
not
get

Short U

Name _____

Cup has the short-**u** sound. This sound is usually spelled by the letter **u**.

c**u**p

Name the pictures. Circle each picture whose name has the short-**u** sound.

bun   cot   duck   bus

bed   lips   sun   bat

rug   bib   log   tub

hog   jug   puppy   six

Short U

Name _____

Name the pictures. Write **u** below each picture whose name has the short-**u** sound.

c**u**p

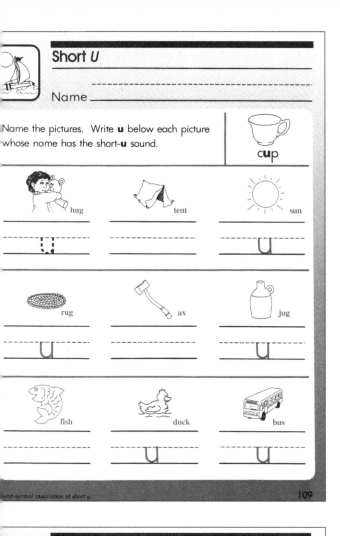

hug	tent	sun
u		u

rug	ax	jug
u		u

fish	duck	bus
	u	u

Short U

Name _____

Read the words and look at the pictures. Draw a line from each word to the picture it tells about.

c**u**p

bus
sun

bun
bug

tub
hug

run
rug

cup
pup

cut
cub

mud
mug

nut
jug

Short U

Name _____

Read each sentence and the words beside it. Write the word that makes sense in each sentence.

c**u**p

1. Jan put the pup into the ___tub___.

cub
tub
cut

2. The cub fell into the ___mud___.

mud
run
nut

3. Dan put the ___cups___ and mugs into a box.

cuts
sun
cups

4. Russ had to ___run___ to get help.

run
tub
mug

5. Lee will fix the ___cut___ on his leg.

cut
jug
sun

6. Pam got the can of ___nuts___ for Mom.

cuts
nuts
mug

REVIEW Short Vowels

Name _____

Read the words and name the pictures. Circle the word that names each picture.

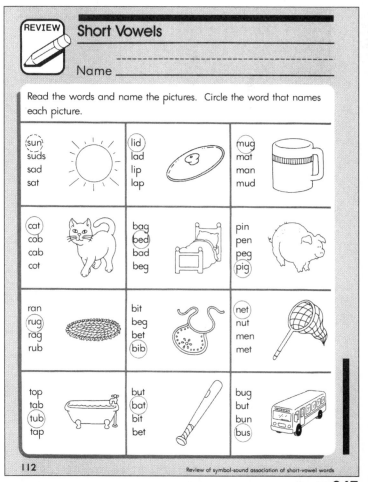

sun suds sad sat		lid lad lip lap		mug mat man mud	
cat cob cab cot		bag bed bad beg		pin pen peg pig	
ran rug rag rub		bit beg bet bib		net nut men met	
top tab tub tap		but bat bit bet		bug but bun bus	

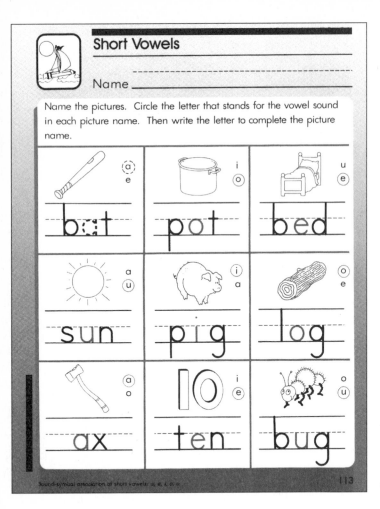

Short Vowels

Name _____

Name the pictures. Circle the letter that stands for the vowel sound in each picture name. Then write the letter to complete the picture name.

(a) e	i o	u (e)
ba t	pot	bed
a (u)	(i) a	o e
sun	pig	log
(a) o	i (e)	o (u)
ax	ten	bug

113

Sound-symbol association of short vowels: a, e, i, o, u

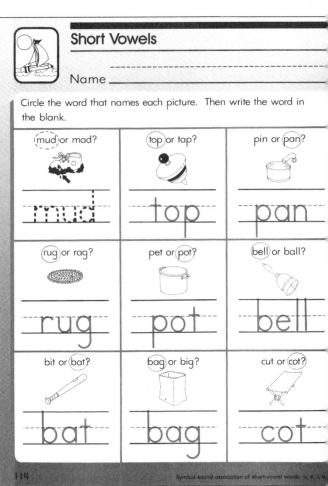

Short Vowels

Name _____

Circle the word that names each picture. Then write the word in the blank.

(mud) or mad?	(top) or tap?	pin or (pan)?
mud	top	pan
(rug) or rag?	pet or (pot)?	(bell) or ball?
rug	pot	bell
bit or (bat)?	(bag) or big?	cut or (cot)?
bat	bag	cot

114

Symbol-sound association of short-vowel words: a, e, i, o, u

Short Vowels

Name _____

In each row, look at the letters and name the pictures. Circle each picture whose name has the short vowel sound the letter stands for.

a	(ant)	hat	nest
e	desk	log	egg
i	ham	pig	pan
o	map	mop	box
u	sun	socks	duck

Symbol-sound association of short vowels: a, e, i, o, u

115

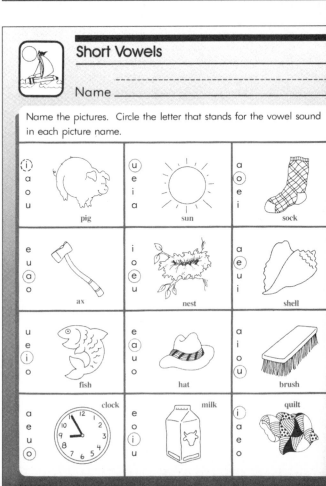

Short Vowels

Name _____

Name the pictures. Circle the letter that stands for the vowel sound in each picture name.

(i) a o u	u e i a	a o e i
pig	sun	sock
e u (a) o	i o e u	a (e) u i
ax	nest	shell
u e (i) o	e (a) u o	a i o (u)
fish	hat	brush
a e u (o)	e o (i) u	(i) a e o
clock	milk	quilt

116

Sound-symbol association of short vowels: a, e, i, o, u

268

Name

Read the sentences and the words under the blanks. Circle the word that belongs in each sentence. Then write the word in the blank.

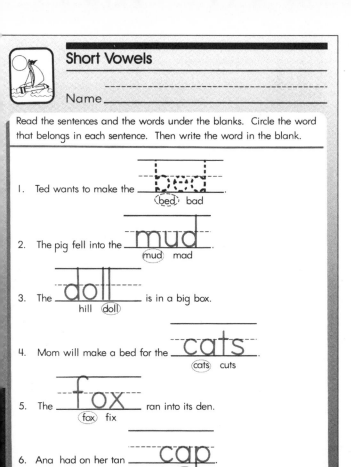

1. Ted wants to make the ___bed___.
   (bed) bad

2. The pig fell into the ___mud___.
   (mud) mad

3. The ___doll___ is in a big box.
   hill (doll)

4. Mom will make a bed for the ___cats___.
   (cats) cuts

5. The ___fox___ ran into its den.
   (fox) fix

6. Ana had on her tan ___cap___.
   cub (cap)

Name

Read the words and look at the pictures. Draw a line from the pictures to the words they tell about.

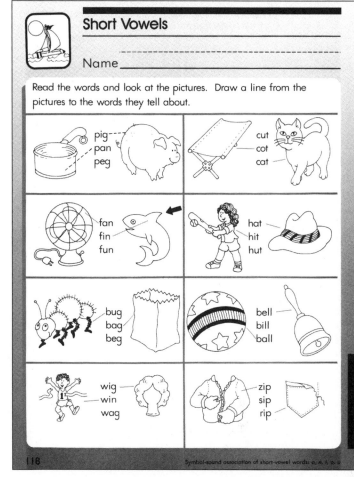

pig
pan
peg

cut
cot
cat

fan
fin
fun

hat
hit
hut

bug
bag
beg

bell
bill
ball

wig
win
wag

zip
sip
rip

Name

Read the sentences and the words under the blanks. Circle the word that belongs in each sentence. Then write the word in the blank.

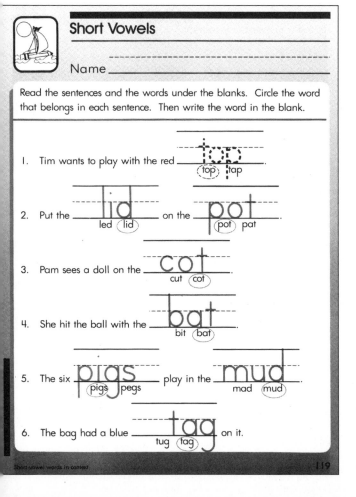

1. Tim wants to play with the red ___top___.
   (top) tap

2. Put the ___lid___ on the ___pot___.
   led (lid)   (pot) pat

3. Pam sees a doll on the ___cot___.
   cut (cot)

4. She hit the ball with the ___bat___.
   bit (bat)

5. The six ___pigs___ play in the ___mud___.
   (pigs) pegs   mad (mud)

6. The bag had a blue ___tag___ on it.
   tug (tag)

Name

Read the sentences and look at the pictures. Draw a line from each sentence to the picture it tells about.

The cat plays with the rag.
The cat plays with the rug.

Dad has the mop.
Dad has the map.

The dog has the bell.
The dog has the ball.

Lin got the bug.
Lin got the bag.

Dan has a red cup.
Dan has a red cap.

Mom will fix the ham.
Mom will fix the hem.

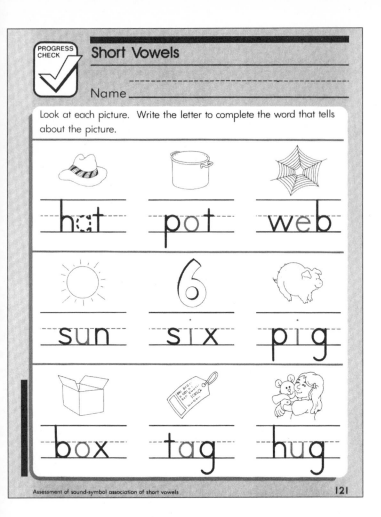

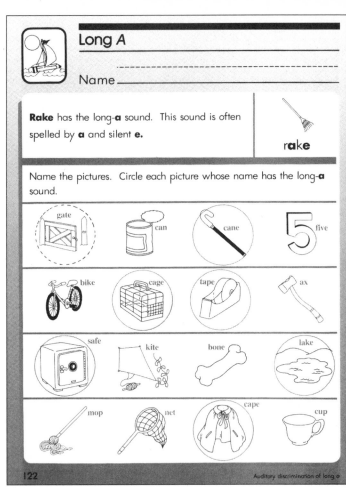

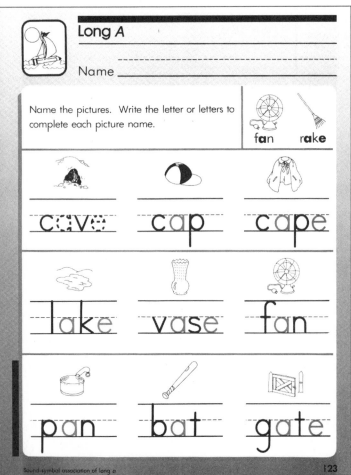

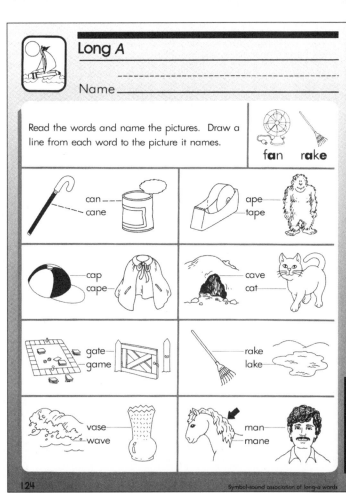

Long A

Name _____

Read each sentence and words beside it. Write the word that makes sense in the sentence.

fan rake

1. Dale ___ate___ the ham.	at / ate / am
2. Is the ___bat___ in the cave?	make / bat / mad
3. Mother wants to fix the ___gate___.	get / gave / gate
4. Did you play the ___game___?	game / gate / gas
5. Jane will fix the pen with ___tape___.	tape / tap / take
6. I have the ___pan___ for the mix.	pan / rake / pat

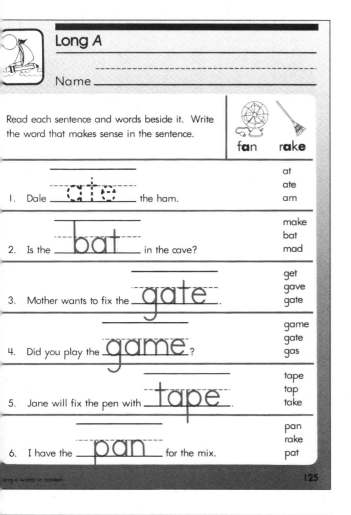

125

Long I

Name _____

Kite has the long-i sound. This sound is often spelled by **i** and silent **e**.

kite

Name the pictures. Circle each picture whose name has the long-i sound.

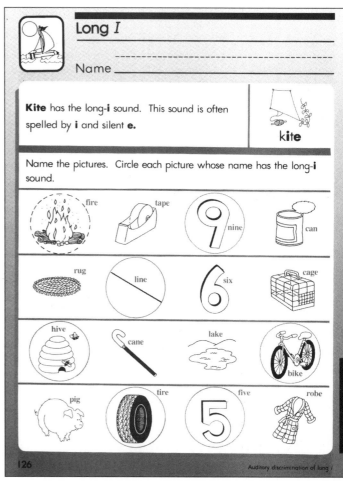

fire   tape   nine   can
rug   line   six   cage
hive   cane   lake   bike
pig   tire   five   robe

126
Auditory discrimination of long i

Long I

Name _____

Read the words and look at the pictures. Draw a line from each word to the picture it tells about.

bib kite

hive / five   line / nine
bike / bite   tire / fire
kites / pipes   vine / pine
ride / wire   dive / dime

Symbol-sound association of long-i words
127

Long I

Name _____

Name the pictures. Write the letter or letters to complete each picture name.

bib kite

line   dime   pig
lid   hive   vine
six   bike   hill

128
Sound-symbol association of long i

Long I

Name _____

Read each sentence and the words beside it. Write the word that makes sense in the sentence.

bi**b**   ki**te**

1. Jill will __dive__ into the lake.		did dive dime
2. Do you like to play with __kites__ ?		kit kites kiss
3. The __hive__ is in the pines.		hive hid hide
4. Kim will __fix__ the tire on the car.		fire fix file
5. I like to hike in the __hills__ .		hive hills hid
6. Mike will __ride__ on his bike.		ripe rid ride

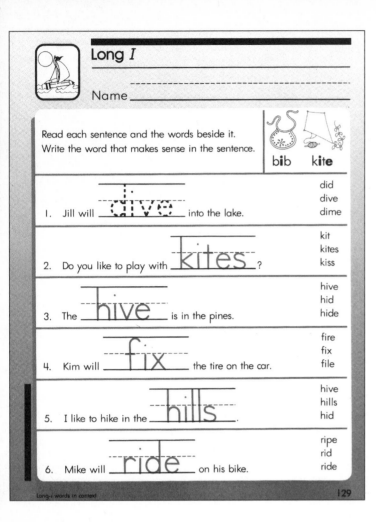

Long A and Long I

Name _____

Read the words and look at the pictures. Circle the word that tells about each picture.

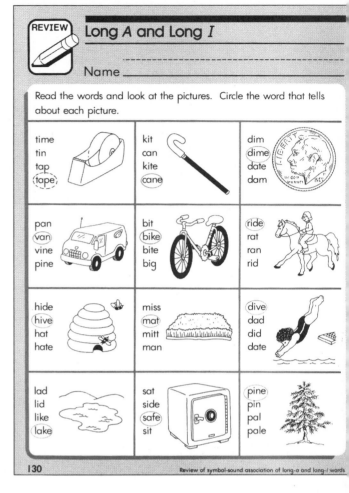

time
tin
tap
(tape)

kit
can
kite
(cane)

dim
(dime)
date
dam

pan
(van)
vine
pine

bit
(bike)
bite
big

(ride)
rat
ran
rid

hide
(hive)
hat
hate

miss
(mat)
mitt
man

(dive)
dad
did
date

lad
lid
like
(lake)

sat
side
(safe)
sit

(pine)
pin
pal
pale

Long O

Name _____

Bone has the long-**o** sound. This sound is often spelled by **o** and silent **e**.

b**o**n**e**

Name the pictures. Circle each picture whose name has the long-**o** sound.

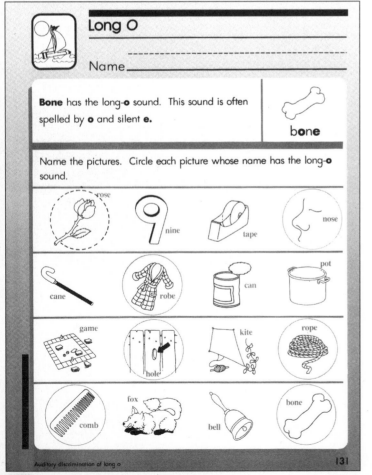

rose   nine   tape   nose

cane   robe   can   pot

game   hole   kite   rope

comb   fox   bell   bone

Long O

Name _____

Read the words and look at the pictures. Draw a line from each word to the picture it tells about.

t**o**p   b**o**ne

rope
vote

poke
pot

home
hop

cone
bone

note
robe

hose
hole

pole
pop

rose
nose

Name _____

Name the pictures. Write the letter or letters to complete each picture name.

t**o**p   b**o**ne

note   rose   fox

robe   mop   cot

top   rope   hole

sound-symbol association of long o   133

Name _____

Read each sentence and the words beside it. Write the word that makes sense in the sentence.

t**o**p   b**o**ne

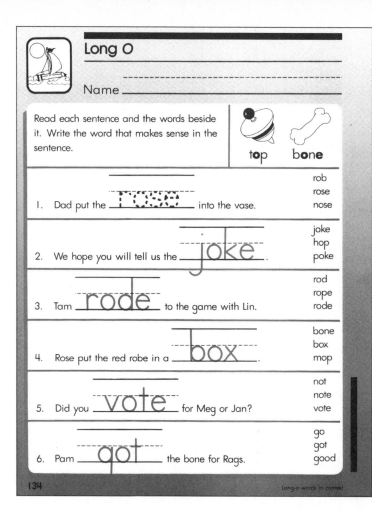

1. Dad put the _____rose_____ into the vase.   rob / rose / nose

2. We hope you will tell us the ___joke___.   joke / hop / poke

3. Tam ___rode___ to the game with Lin.   rod / rope / rode

4. Rose put the red robe in a ___box___.   bone / box / mop

5. Did you ___vote___ for Meg or Jan?   not / note / vote

6. Pam ___got___ the bone for Rags.   go / got / good

134   Long-o words in context

Name _____

Tube has the long-**u** sound. This sound is often spelled by **u** and silent **e**.

t**u**be

Name the pictures. Circle each picture whose name has the long-**u** sound.

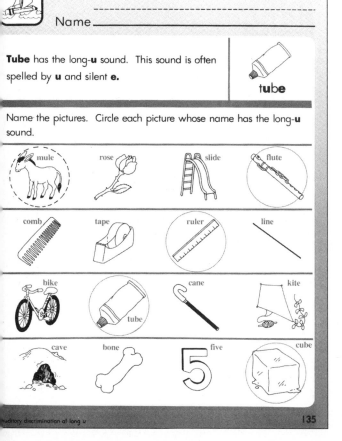

mule   rose   slide   flute

comb   tape   ruler   line

bike   tube   cane   kite

cave   bone   5 five   cube

auditory discrimination of long u   135

Name _____

Read the words and look at the pictures. Draw a line from each word to the picture it tells about.

c**u**p   t**u**be

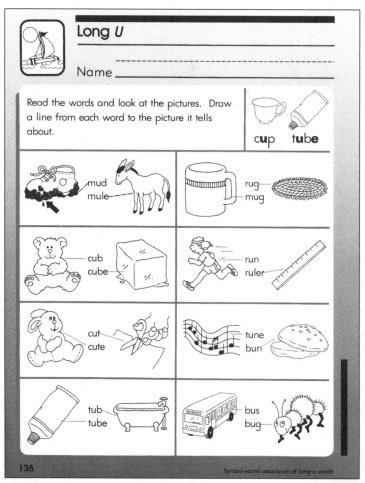

mud / mule   rug / mug

cub / cube   run / ruler

cut / cute   tune / bun

tub / tube   bus / bug

136   Symbol-sound association of long-u words

273

Long *U*

Name _____

Look at each picture. Write the letter or letters to complete the word that tells about the picture.

cup tube

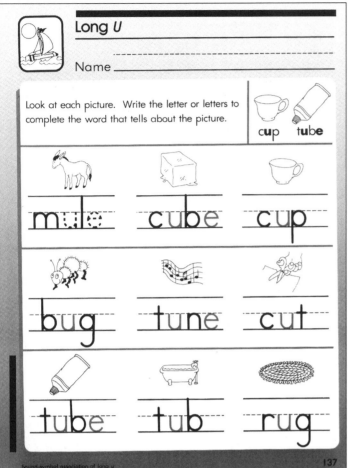

mule	cube	cup
bug	tune	cut
tube	tub	rug

Sound-symbol association of long *u* 137

Long *U*

Name _____

Read each sentence and the words beside it. Write the word that makes sense in the sentence.

cup tube

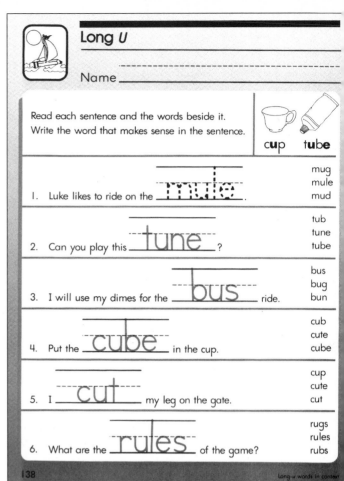

1. Luke likes to ride on the __mule__.
   - mug
   - mule
   - mud

2. Can you play this __tune__?
   - tub
   - tune
   - tube

3. I will use my dimes for the __bus__ ride.
   - bus
   - bug
   - bun

4. Put the __cube__ in the cup.
   - cub
   - cute
   - cube

5. I __cut__ my leg on the gate.
   - cup
   - cute
   - cut

6. What are the __rules__ of the game?
   - rugs
   - rules
   - rubs

138 Long-*u* words in context

REVIEW Long O and Long *U*

Name _____

Read the words and name the pictures. Circle the word that names each picture.

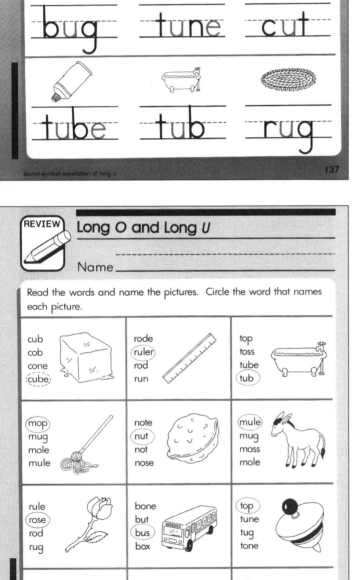

cub cob cone (cube)	rode (ruler) rod run	top toss tube (tub)
(mop) mug mole mule	note (nut) not nose	(mule) mug moss mole
rule (rose) rod rug	bone but (bus) box	(top) tune tug tone
rule run (rope) rot	(bone) box bus bun	(note) nut nose not

Review of symbol-sound association of long-*o* and long-*u* words 139

REVIEW Long Vowels

Name _____

Name the pictures. Write the letters to complete each picture name.

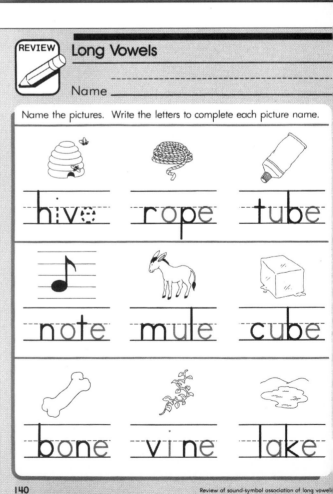

hive	rope	tube
note	mule	cube
bone	vine	lake

140 Review of sound-symbol association of long vowels

274

Long Vowels

Name _____

Read each sentence and the words beside it. Write the word that makes sense in the sentence.

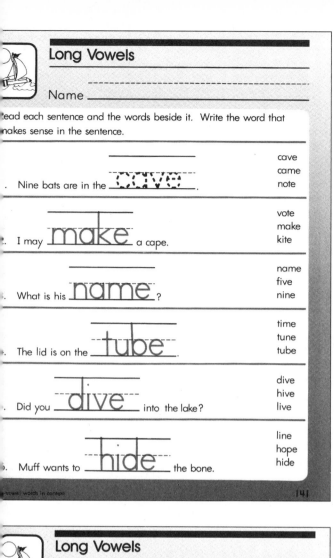

1. Nine bats are in the __cave__ .

cave
came
note

2. I may __make__ a cape.

vote
make
kite

3. What is his __name__ ?

name
five
nine

4. The lid is on the __tube__ .

time
tune
tube

5. Did you __dive__ into the lake?

dive
hive
live

6. Muff wants to __hide__ the bone.

line
hope
hide

141

Long Vowels

Name _____

Circle the word that tells about each picture. Then write the word in the blank.

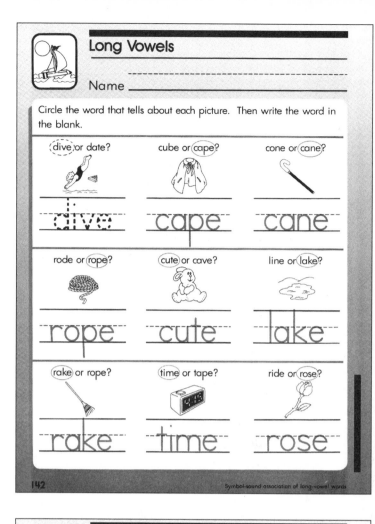

dive or date? __dive__

cube or cape? __cape__

cone or cane? __cane__

rode or rope? __rope__

cute or cave? __cute__

line or lake? __lake__

rake or rope? __rake__

time or tape? __time__

ride or rose? __rose__

142

Long Vowels

Name _____

Read the sentences and name the pictures. Write the word that names each picture.

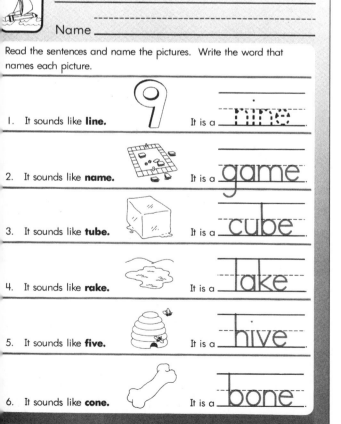

1. It sounds like **line.** It is a __nine__ .

2. It sounds like **name.** It is a __game__ .

3. It sounds like **tube.** It is a __cube__ .

4. It sounds like **rake.** It is a __lake__ .

5. It sounds like **five.** It is a __hive__ .

6. It sounds like **cone.** It is a __bone__ .

143

Long Vowels

Name _____

Read the words below. Then name the pictures. Write the word that names each picture.

nine	tube	note
wave	rake	hive
bone	bike	cube

__tube__   __nine__   __cube__

__hive__   __wave__   __rake__

__note__   __bike__   __bone__

144

275

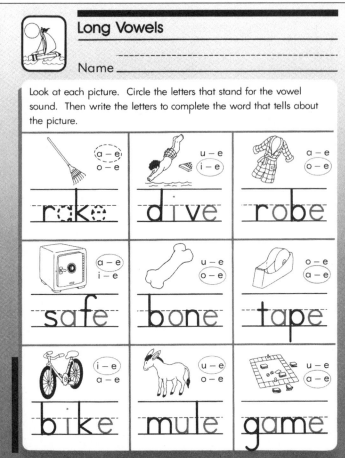

Long Vowels

Name

Look at each picture. Circle the letters that stand for the vowel sound. Then write the letters to complete the word that tells about the picture.

(a – e) o – e rake	u – e (i – e) dive	a – e (o – e) robe
(a – e) i – e safe	u – e (o – e) bone	(o – e) a – e tape
(i – e) a – e bike	u – e o – e mule	u – e (a – e) game

Sound-symbol association of long vowels   145

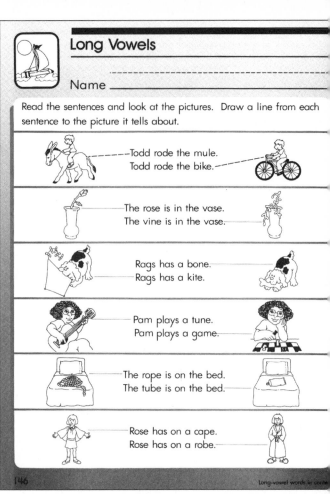

Long Vowels

Name

Read the sentences and look at the pictures. Draw a line from each sentence to the picture it tells about.

Todd rode the mule.
Todd rode the bike.

The rose is in the vase.
The vine is in the vase.

Rags has a bone.
Rags has a kite.

Pam plays a tune.
Pam plays a game.

The rope is on the bed.
The tube is on the bed.

Rose has on a cape.
Rose has on a robe.

146   Long-vowel words in context

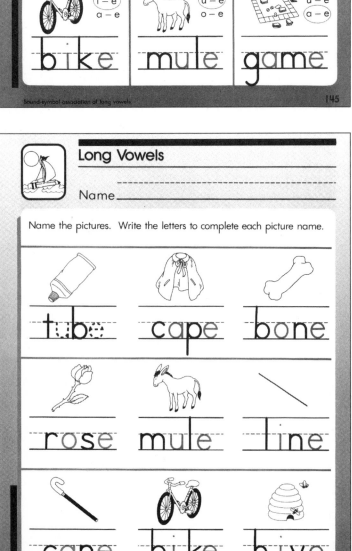

Long Vowels

Name

Name the pictures. Write the letters to complete each picture name.

tube	cape	bone
rose	mule	line
cane	bike	hive

Sound-symbol association of long vowels   147

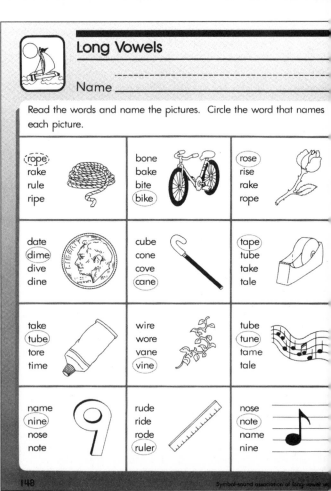

Long Vowels

Name

Read the words and name the pictures. Circle the word that names each picture.

(rope) rake rule ripe	bone bake bite (bike)	(rose) rise rake rope
date (dime) dive dine	cube cone cove (cane)	(tape) tube take tale
take (tube) tore time	wire wore vane (vine)	tube (tune) tame tale
name (nine) nose note	rude ride rode (ruler)	nose (note) name nine

148   Symbol-sound association of long-vowel words

276

Read the sentences and name the pictures. Write the word that names each picture.

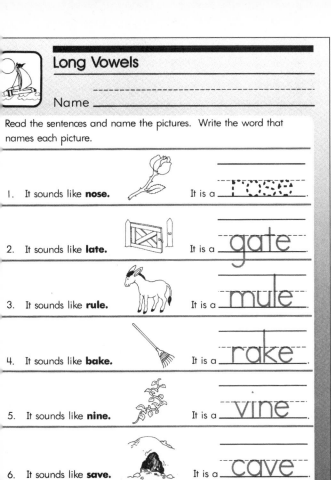

1. It sounds like **nose.** It is a ___rose___.

2. It sounds like **late.** It is a ___gate___.

3. It sounds like **rule.** It is a ___mule___.

4. It sounds like **bake.** It is a ___rake___.

5. It sounds like **nine.** It is a ___vine___.

6. It sounds like **save.** It is a ___cave___.

Name the pictures. Write the letters to complete each picture name.

tune   nine   kite

lake   tape   rope

vine   mule   robe

Name the pictures. Write the letter or letters to complete each picture name.

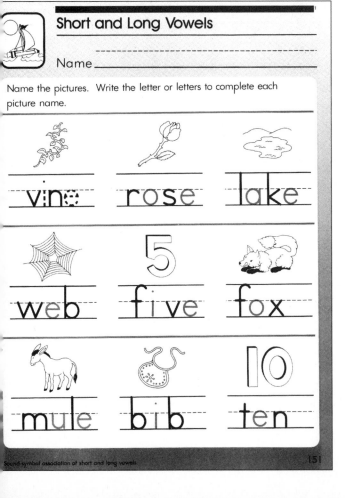

vine   rose   lake

web   five   fox

mule   bib   ten

Read the words and name the pictures. Draw lines from the words to the pictures they name.

pan
pale
pad

nose
not
note

cat
cave
came

rose
robe
rob

bike
bib
bite

cube
cut
cub

man
mane
map

pine
pig
pin

Short and Long Vowels

Name _____

Read each sentence and the words beside it. Write the word that makes sense in the sentence.

1. Did you ride the ____bike____?
   - bit
   - bite
   - bike

2. Put on the red ____robe____.
   - rob
   - rug
   - robe

3. Tell Jane to ____fix____ the kite.
   - fix
   - fox
   - five

4. I have ____nine____ dimes to save.
   - net
   - nine
   - name

5. The ____fox____ ran into the den.
   - fat
   - fox
   - fine

6. Put the ____lid____ on the pot.
   - lid
   - like
   - line

Short- and long-vowel words in context

153

Short and Long Vowels

Name _____

Read the sentences and name the pictures. Write the word that names each picture.

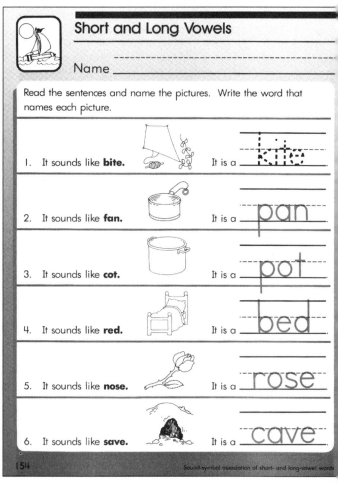

1. It sounds like **bite.** It is a ____kite____.

2. It sounds like **fan.** It is a ____pan____.

3. It sounds like **cot.** It is a ____pot____.

4. It sounds like **red.** It is a ____bed____.

5. It sounds like **nose.** It is a ____rose____.

6. It sounds like **save.** It is a ____cave____.

154

Sound-symbol association of short- and long-vowel words

Short and Long Vowels

Name _____

Read the words below. Then name the pictures. Write the word that names each picture.

nine	rose	bat
pig	hive	cube
box	cane	sun

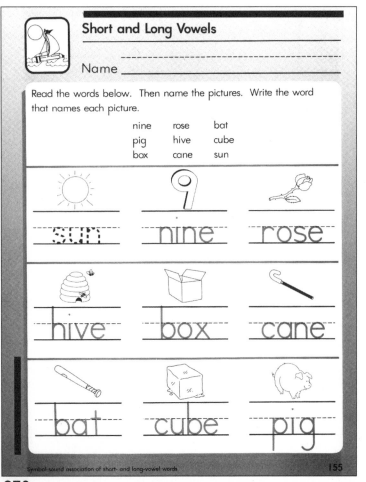

____sun____   ____nine____   ____rose____

____hive____   ____box____   ____cane____

____bat____   ____cube____   ____pig____

Symbol-sound association of short- and long-vowel words

155

Short and Long Vowels

Parent Involvement Master 2, Page T–42

Name _____

Read the sentences and look at the pictures. Draw a line from each sentence to the picture it tells about.

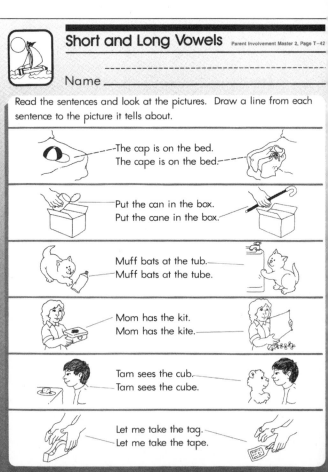

The cap is on the bed.
The cape is on the bed.

Put the can in the box.
Put the cane in the box.

Muff bats at the tub.
Muff bats at the tube.

Mom has the kit.
Mom has the kite.

Tam sees the cub.
Tam sees the cube.

Let me take the tag.
Let me take the tape.

156

Short- and long-vowel words in context

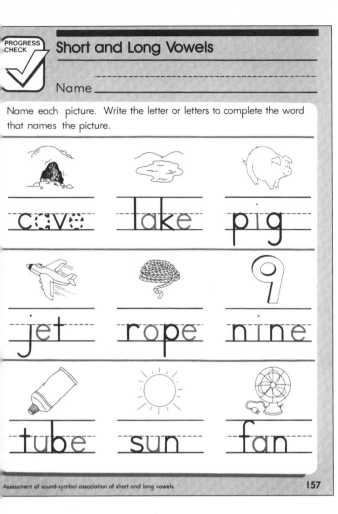

Short and Long Vowels

Name _____

Name each picture. Write the letter or letters to complete the word that names the picture.

cave　　　lake　　　pig

jet　　　rope　　　nine

tube　　　sun　　　fan

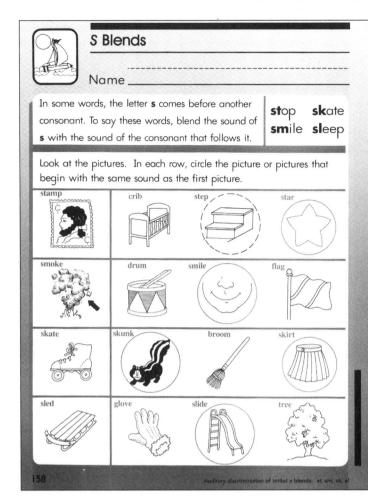

S Blends

Name _____

In some words, the letter **s** comes before another consonant. To say these words, blend the sound of **s** with the sound of the consonant that follows it.

stop	**sk**ate
smile	**sl**eep

Look at the pictures. In each row, circle the picture or pictures that begin with the same sound as the first picture.

stamp	crib	step	star
smoke	drum	smile	flag
skate	skunk	broom	skirt
sled	glove	slide	tree

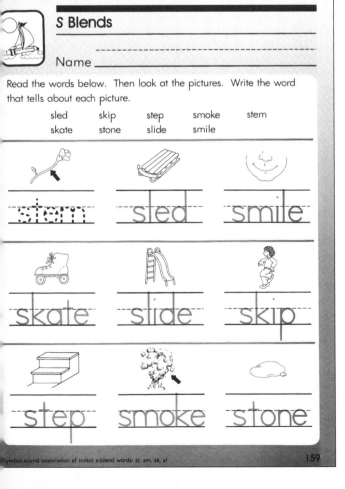

S Blends

Name _____

Read the words below. Then look at the pictures. Write the word that tells about each picture.

sled	skip	step	smoke	stem
skate	stone	slide	smile	

stem　　　sled　　　smile

skate　　　slide　　　skip

step　　　smoke　　　stone

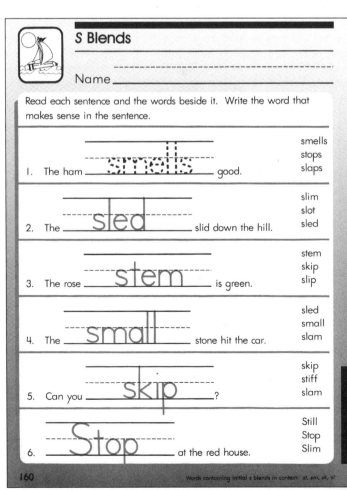

S Blends

Name _____

Read each sentence and the words beside it. Write the word that makes sense in the sentence.

1. The ham _____smells_____ good.　smells / stops / slaps

2. The _____sled_____ slid down the hill.　slim / slot / sled

3. The rose _____stem_____ is green.　stem / skip / slip

4. The _____small_____ stone hit the car.　sled / small / slam

5. Can you _____skip_____ ?　skip / stiff / slam

6. _____Stop_____ at the red house.　Still / Stop / Slim

S Blends

Name _____

In some words, the letter **s** comes before another consonant. To say these words, blend the sound of **s** with the sound of the consonant that follows it.

scare **snap**
swim **spin**

Look at the pictures. In each row, circle the picture or pictures that begin with the same sound as the first picture.

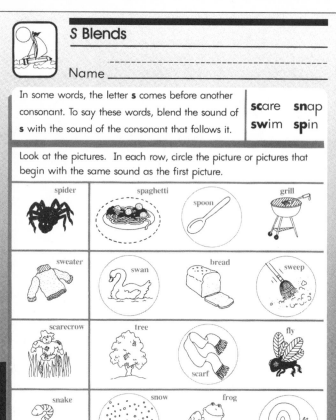

S Blends

Name _____

Read the words below. Then look at the pictures. Write the word that tells about each picture.

spill   snake   scale   snip   spell
snap   scare   swim   spin

S Blends

Name _____

Read each sentence and the words beside it. Write the word that makes sense in the sentence.

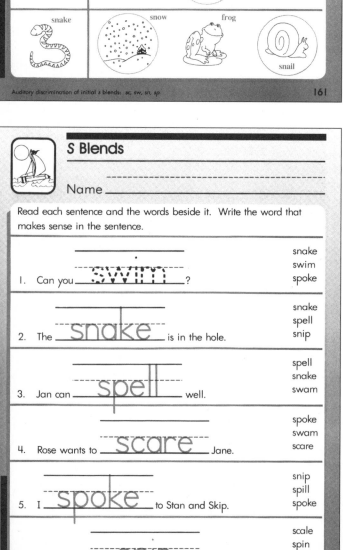

1. Can you **swim**?
   - snake
   - swim
   - spoke

2. The **snake** is in the hole.
   - snake
   - spell
   - snip

3. Jan can **spell** well.
   - spell
   - snake
   - swam

4. Rose wants to **scare** Jane.
   - spoke
   - swam
   - scare

5. I **spoke** to Stan and Skip.
   - snip
   - spill
   - spoke

6. Can the top **spin**?
   - scale
   - spin
   - spoke

REVIEW

S Blends

Name _____

Read the words and look at the pictures. Circle the word that tells about each picture.

slim
(skip)
snip
swim

smell
swell
spell
still

spine
smile
skid
(slide)

spoke
(stone)
smoke
slope

(swim)
slim
spin
skin

stop
slap
skip
(snap)

(spill)
swell
smell
still

snake
state
(scale)
spare

(spin)
skin
slim
swim

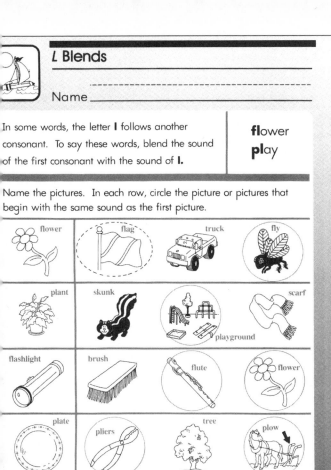

L Blends

Name_____

In some words, the letter **l** follows another consonant. To say these words, blend the sound of the first consonant with the sound of **l**.

flower
play

Name the pictures. In each row, circle the picture or pictures that begin with the same sound as the first picture.

flower	flag	truck	fly
plant	skunk	playground	scarf
flashlight	brush	flute	flower
plate	pliers	tree	plow

L Blends

Name_____

Read the words below. Then look at the pictures. Write the word that tells about each picture.

play	plate	flag	flute	plane
plug	flame	flat	plum	

flute	flag	plate
flame	play	plug
plum	plane	flat

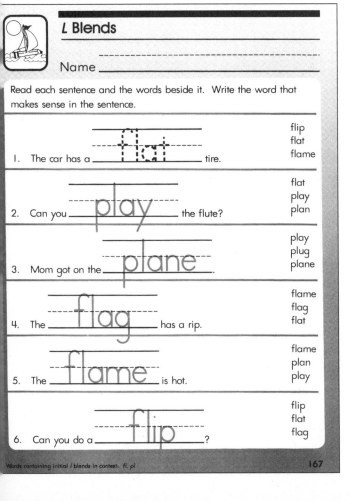

L Blends

Name_____

Read each sentence and the words beside it. Write the word that makes sense in the sentence.

1. The car has a __flat__ tire.

   flip
   flat
   flame

2. Can you __play__ the flute?

   flat
   play
   plan

3. Mom got on the __plane__.

   play
   plug
   plane

4. The __flag__ has a rip.

   flame
   flag
   flat

5. The __flame__ is hot.

   flame
   plan
   play

6. Can you do a __flip__?

   flip
   flat
   flag

L Blends

Name_____

In some words, the letter **l** follows another consonant. To say these words, blend the sound of the first consonant with the sound of **l**.

clown
blue
glad

Look at the pictures. In each row, circle the picture or pictures that begin with the same sound as the first picture.

clock	clap	fly	cloud
glass	snake	globe	glove
blanket	block	dress	train
clown	clock	climb	spaghetti

L Blends

Name _____

Read the words below. Then look at the pictures. Write the word that tells about each picture.

clip	blade	globe	clam	glass
club	clap	class	glad	

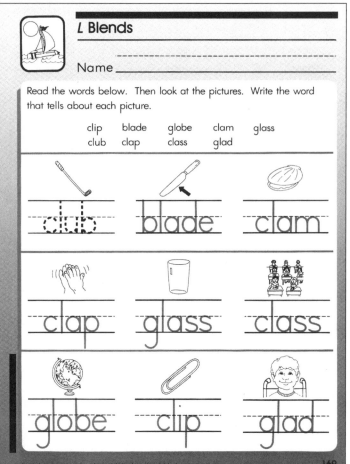

club   blade   clam

clap   glass   class

globe   clip   glad

L Blends

Name _____

Read each sentence and the words beside it. Write the word that makes sense in the sentence.

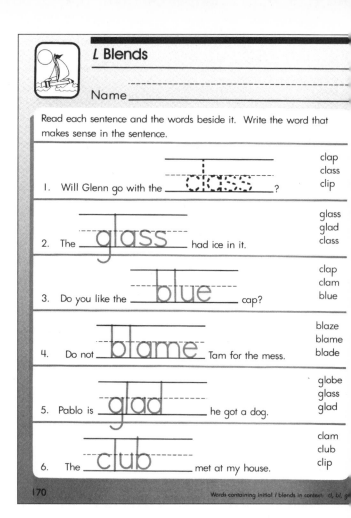

1. Will Glenn go with the ____class____ ?

   clap / class / clip

2. The ____glass____ had ice in it.

   glass / glad / class

3. Do you like the ____blue____ cap?

   clap / clam / blue

4. Do not ____blame____ Tam for the mess.

   blaze / blame / blade

5. Pablo is ____glad____ he got a dog.

   globe / glass / glad

6. The ____club____ met at my house.

   clam / club / clip

L Blends

Name _____

Read the words and name the pictures. Circle the word that names each picture.

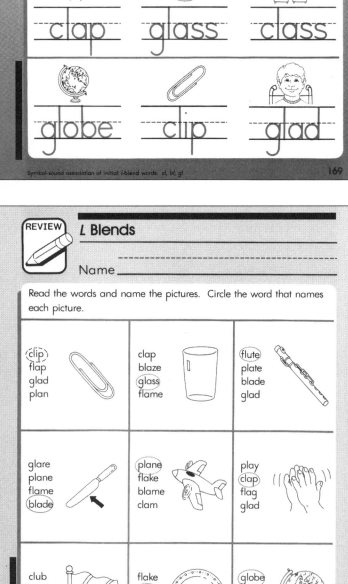

(clip) flap glad plan	clap blaze (glass) flame	(flute) plate blade glad
glare plane flame (blade)	(plane) flake blame clam	play (clap) flag glad
club plug (flag) glad	flake (plate) blame glare	(globe) blob club plug

---

R Blends

Name _____

In some words, the letter **r** follows another consonant. To say these words, blend the sound of the first consonant with the sound of **r**.

frog
brown
green

Name the pictures. In each row, circle the pictures that begin with the same sound as the first picture.

frog	fruit	spoon	frame
broom	squirrel	brick	brush
grass	grill	grapes	dress
bread	bridge	bracelet	fly

R Blends

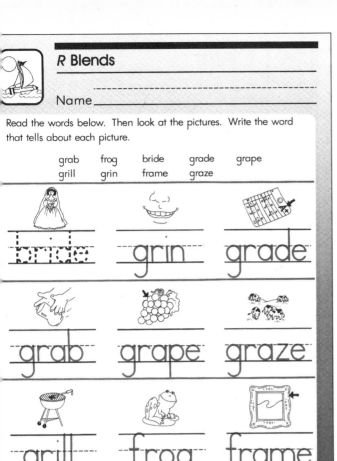

Name _____

Read the words below. Then look at the pictures. Write the word that tells about each picture.

grab	frog	bride	grade	grape
grill	grin	frame	graze	

bride   grin   grade

grab   grape   graze

grill   frog   frame

R Blends

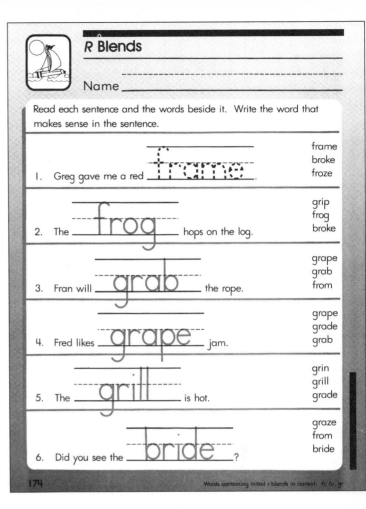

Name _____

Read each sentence and the words beside it. Write the word that makes sense in the sentence.

1. Greg gave me a red __frame__ . frame / broke / froze

2. The __frog__ hops on the log. grip / frog / broke

3. Fran will __grab__ the rope. grape / grab / from

4. Fred likes __grape__ jam. grape / grade / grab

5. The __grill__ is hot. grin / grill / grade

6. Did you see the __bride__ ? graze / from / bride

R Blends

Name _____

In some words, the letter **r** follows another consonant. To say these words, blend the sound of the first consonant with the sound of **r**.

cry **pr**etty
dress **tr**ee

Look at the pictures. In each row, circle the picture or pictures that begin with the same sound as the first picture.

crab	crack	blanket	crayon
dress	frog	dragon	drill
present	brick	grapes	prize
tree	train	truck	slide

R Blends

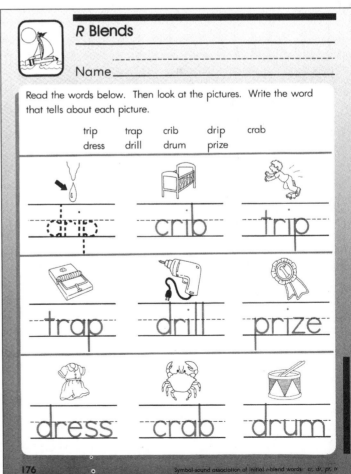

Name _____

Read the words below. Then look at the pictures. Write the word that tells about each picture.

trip	trap	crib	drip	crab
dress	drill	drum	prize	

drip   crib   trip

trap   drill   prize

dress   crab   drum

283

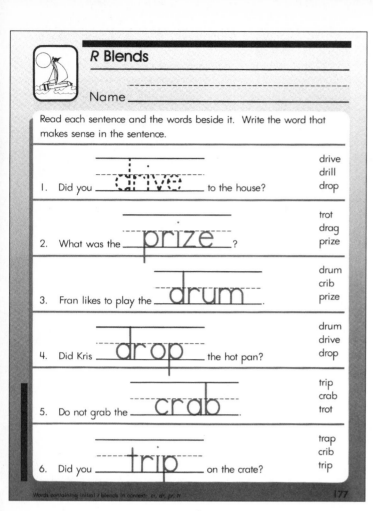

R Blends

Name_____

Read each sentence and the words beside it. Write the word that makes sense in the sentence.

1. Did you **drive** to the house? — drive / drill / drop

2. What was the **prize**? — trot / drag / prize

3. Fran likes to play the **drum**. — drum / crib / prize

4. Did Kris **drop** the hot pan? — drum / drive / drop

5. Do not grab the **crab**. — trip / crab / trot

6. Did you **trip** on the crate? — trap / crib / trip

Words containing initial r blends in context: cr, dr, pr, tr — 177

REVIEW R Blends

Name_____

Read the words and look at the pictures. Circle the word that tells about each picture.

grapes (circled) / brave / trade / frames	from / drum (circled) / grab / crate	grill / drip / crib / trap (circled)
crab (circled) / grass / trap / drag	prize / bride (circled) / drive / trade	drag / frog (circled) / crop / grab
prize / bride / froze / drive (circled)	grin (circled) / trim / drum / from	graze / prize (circled) / prune / bride

178 — Review of symbol-sound association of initial r-blend words: fr, br, gr, cr, dr, pr

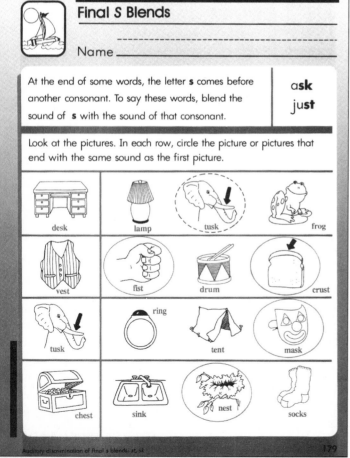

Final S Blends

Name_____

At the end of some words, the letter **s** comes before another consonant. To say these words, blend the sound of **s** with the sound of that consonant.

as**k**
jus**t**

Look at the pictures. In each row, circle the picture or pictures that end with the same sound as the first picture.

desk | lamp | tusk | frog

vest | fist | drum | crust

tusk | ring | tent | mask

chest | sink | nest | socks

Auditory discrimination of final s blends: st, sk — 179

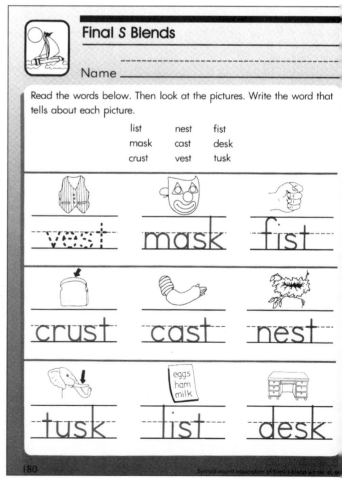

Final S Blends

Name_____

Read the words below. Then look at the pictures. Write the word that tells about each picture.

list   nest   fist
mask   cast   desk
crust   vest   tusk

vest | **mask** | **fist**

crust | **cast** | **nest**

tusk | **list** | **desk**

180 — Symbol-sound association of final s-blend words: st, sk

284

Final S Blends

Name _____

Read each sentence and the words beside it. Write the word that makes sense in the sentence.

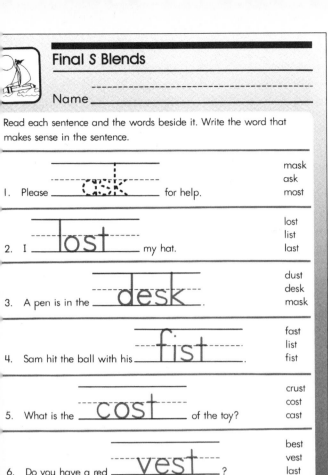

1. Please __ask__ for help.

    mask
    ask
    most

2. I __lost__ my hat.

    lost
    list
    last

3. A pen is in the __desk__.

    dust
    desk
    mask

4. Sam hit the ball with his __fist__.

    fast
    list
    fist

5. What is the __cost__ of the toy?

    crust
    cost
    cast

6. Do you have a red __vest__?

    best
    vest
    last

Words containing final s blends in context: *st, sk*   181

Final S Blends

Parent Involvement Master 3, Page T-43

Name _____

Read the words and look at the pictures. Circle the word that tells about each picture.

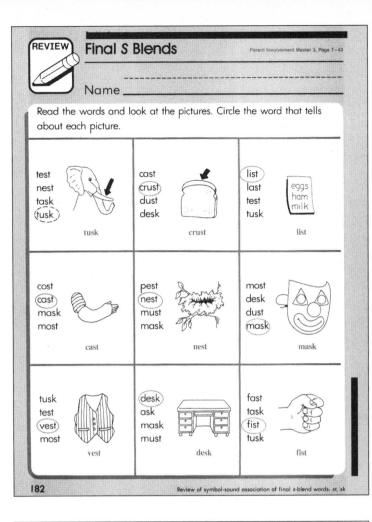

test nest task (tusk)	cast (crust) dust desk	(list) last test tusk
tusk	crust	list
cost (cast) mask most	(pest) (nest) must mask	most desk dust (mask)
cast	nest	mask
tusk test (vest) most	(desk) ask mask must	fast task (fist) tusk
vest	desk	fist

182   Review of symbol-sound association of final s-blend words: *st, sk*

Blends

Name _____

Read the words below. Then look at the pictures. Write the word that tells about each picture.

drum   sled   desk   flag   snake
crab   nest   plate   frog

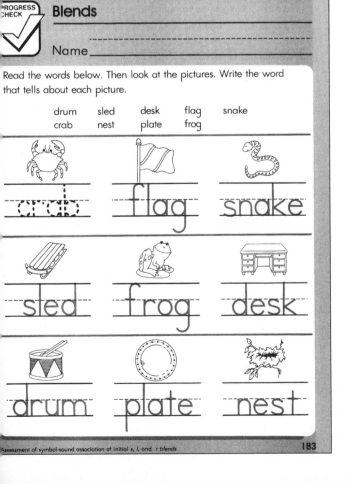

crab   flag   snake

sled   frog   desk

drum   plate   nest

Assessment of symbol-sound association of initial s, l, and r blends   183

Vowel Pairs: *AI* and *AY*

Name _____

Train has the long-**a** sound spelled **ai**. **Hay** has the long-**a** sound spelled **ay**.

train   hay

Read the words and look at the pictures. Circle the word that tells about each picture.

(rain) ray	train (tray)	mail (nail)
(sail) say	plain (play)	(mail) may
(snail) sail	tray (trail)	brain (braid)
(rail) ray	(tail) trail	claim (clay)

184   Symbol-sound association of words containing vowel digraphs: *ai, ay*

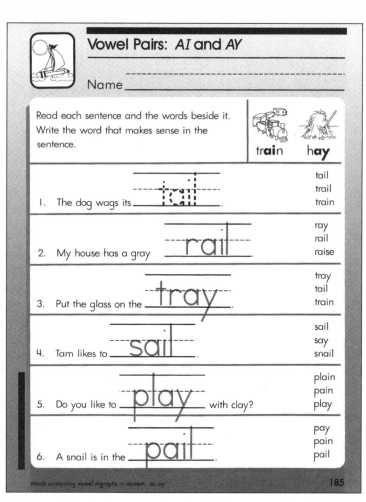

Vowel Pairs: *AI* and *AY*

Name _____

Read each sentence and the words beside it. Write the word that makes sense in the sentence.

train **hay**

1.	The dog wags its ___tail___ .	tail trail train
2.	My house has a gray ___rail___ .	ray rail raise
3.	Put the glass on the ___tray___ .	tray tail train
4.	Tam likes to ___sail___ .	sail say snail
5.	Do you like to ___play___ with clay?	plain pain play
6.	A snail is in the ___pail___ .	pay pain pail

Words containing vowel digraphs in context: *ai, ay*   185

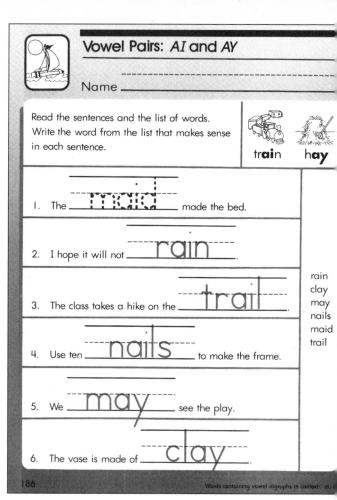

Vowel Pairs: *AI* and *AY*

Name _____

Read the sentences and the list of words. Write the word from the list that makes sense in each sentence.

train **hay**

1.	The ___maid___ made the bed.
2.	I hope it will not ___rain___ .
3.	The class takes a hike on the ___trail___ .
4.	Use ten ___nails___ to make the frame.
5.	We ___may___ see the play.
6.	The vase is made of ___clay___ .

rain
clay
may
nails
maid
trail

186   Words containing vowel digraphs in context: *ai, a*

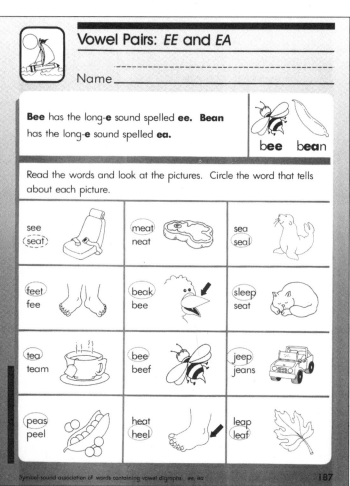

Vowel Pairs: *EE* and *EA*

Name _____

Bee has the long-**e** sound spelled **ee**. **Bean** has the long-**e** sound spelled **ea**.

bee **bean**

Read the words and look at the pictures. Circle the word that tells about each picture.

see (seat)	(meat) neat	sea (seal)
(feet) fee	(beak) bee	(sleep) seat
(tea) team	(bee) beef	(jeep) jeans
(peas) peel	heat (heel)	leap (leaf)

Symbol-sound association of words containing vowel digraphs: *ee, ea*   187

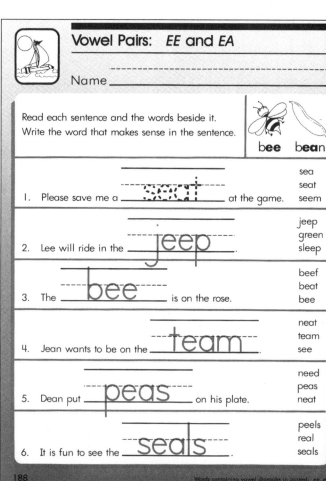

Vowel Pairs: *EE* and *EA*

Name _____

Read each sentence and the words beside it. Write the word that makes sense in the sentence.

bee **bean**

1.	Please save me a ___seat___ at the game.	sea seat seem
2.	Lee will ride in the ___jeep___ .	jeep green sleep
3.	The ___bee___ is on the rose.	beef beat bee
4.	Jean wants to be on the ___team___ .	neat team see
5.	Dean put ___peas___ on his plate.	need peas neat
6.	It is fun to see the ___seals___ .	peels real seals

188   Words containing vowel digraphs in context: *ee, e*

286

Vowel Pairs: *EE* and *EA*

Name _____

Read the sentences and the list of words. Write the word from the list that makes sense in each sentence.

bee   bean

1. Dee will __need__ a hat.

2. Do you want to eat the __meat__?

3. The __tree__ will be cut down.

4. The grass feels good on my __feet__.

5. Neal keeps his home __neat__.

6. The __sea__ is deep and blue.

neat
need
sea
tree
meat
feet

Name _____

Read the words and look at the pictures. Circle the word that tells about each picture.

sail say (seal) see	pay (pail) peel peas	bee beat beak beef
tail team (tea) tray	(mail) may meat meet	ray (rain) read real
(play) pay pain pail	train tray rain (tree)	hay heat heel hail

---

Vowel Pairs: *OA* and *OW*

Name _____

Coat has the long-**o** sound spelled **oa**.
Window has the long-**o** sound spelled **ow**.

c**oa**t   wind**ow**

Read the words and look at the pictures. Circle the word that tells about each picture.

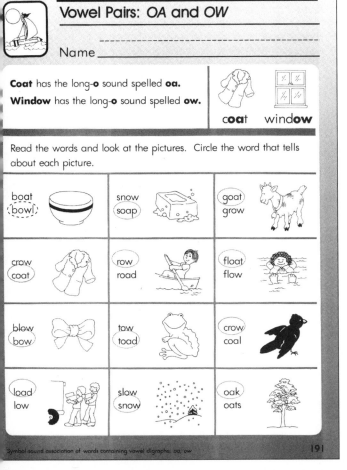

boat (bowl)	snow (soap)	(goat) grow
crow (coat)	(row) road	float flow
blow (bow)	tow (toad)	crow coal
(load) low	slow (snow)	oak (oats)

Vowel Pairs: *OA* and *OW*

Name _____

Read each sentence and the words beside it. Write the word that makes sense in the sentence.

c**oa**t   wind**ow**

1. May I please __row__ the boat?

2. Feed the oats to the __goat__.

3. My __coat__ has a hole in it.

4. The __toad__ sat on a leaf.

5. Mother wants to __load__ the car.

6. Jeff put the peas into a __bowl__.

goat
row
oak

snow
goat
bow

snow
load
coat

bow
toad
row

low
loaf
load

snow
bowl
soap

287

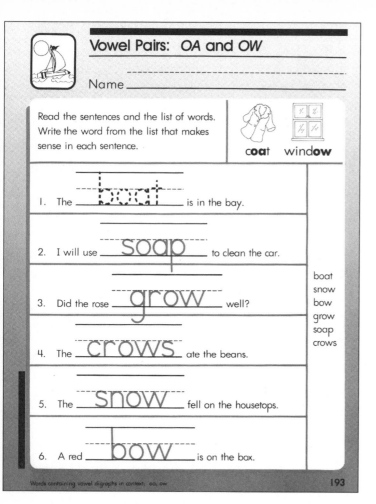

Vowel Pairs: OA and OW

Name _____

Read the sentences and the list of words. Write the word from the list that makes sense in each sentence.

coat   window

1. The **boat** is in the bay.

2. I will use **soap** to clean the car.

3. Did the rose **grow** well?

4. The **crows** ate the beans.

5. The **snow** fell on the housetops.

6. A red **bow** is on the box.

boat
snow
bow
grow
soap
crows

Words containing vowel digraphs in context: oa, ow   193

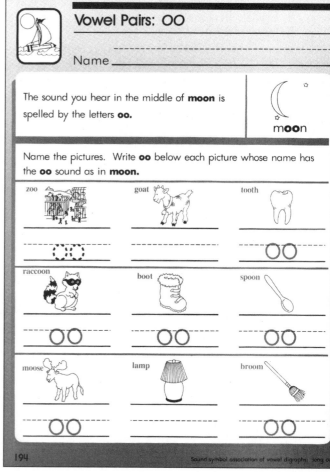

Vowel Pairs: OO

Name _____

The sound you hear in the middle of **moon** is spelled by the letters **oo**.

moon

Name the pictures. Write **oo** below each picture whose name has the **oo** sound as in **moon**.

zoo	goat	tooth
oo		oo

raccoon	boot	spoon
oo	oo	oo

moose	lamp	broom
oo		oo

194   Sound-symbol association of vowel digraphs: long oo

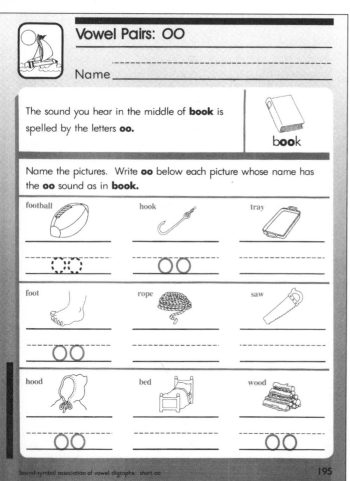

Vowel Pairs: OO

Name _____

The sound you hear in the middle of **book** is spelled by the letters **oo**.

book

Name the pictures. Write **oo** below each picture whose name has the **oo** sound as in **book**.

football	hook	tray
oo	oo	

foot	rope	saw
oo		

hood	bed	wood
oo		oo

Sound-symbol association of vowel digraphs: short oo   195

Vowel Pairs: OO

Name _____

Read the words and name the pictures. Draw a line from each word to the picture it names.

moon   book

food
foot

pool
roof

zoo
woods

moose
hood

book
boot

spoon
spool

hook
stool

broom
brook

196   Symbol-sound association of words containing vowel digraphs: long and short oo

---

288

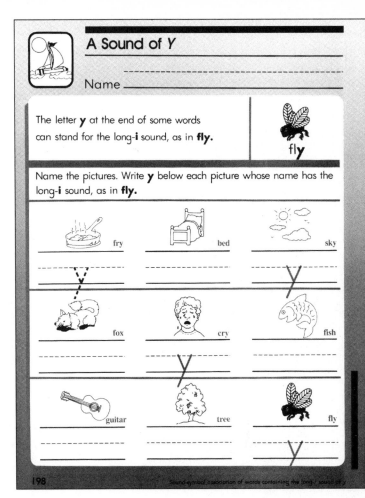

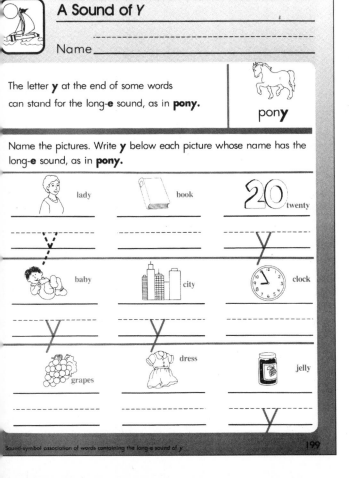

Two Sounds of Y

Name

Read each sentence and the words beside it. Write the word that makes sense in each sentence.

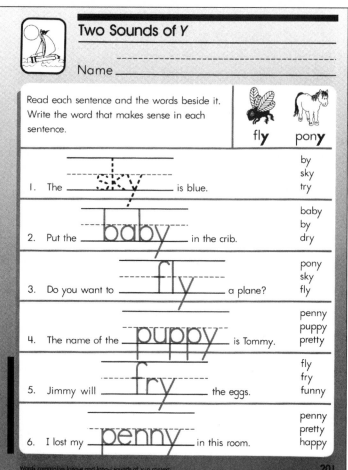

fly **pony**

1. The ___sky___ is blue.

   by
   sky
   try

2. Put the ___baby___ in the crib.

   baby
   by
   dry

3. Do you want to ___fly___ a plane?

   pony
   sky
   fly

4. The name of the ___puppy___ is Tommy.

   penny
   puppy
   pretty

5. Jimmy will ___fry___ the eggs.

   fly
   fry
   funny

6. I lost my ___penny___ in this room.

   penny
   pretty
   happy

Words containing long-e and long-i sounds of y in context

201

Vowel Pairs and Sounds of Y

Name

Read the words and name the picture. Circle the word that names each picture.

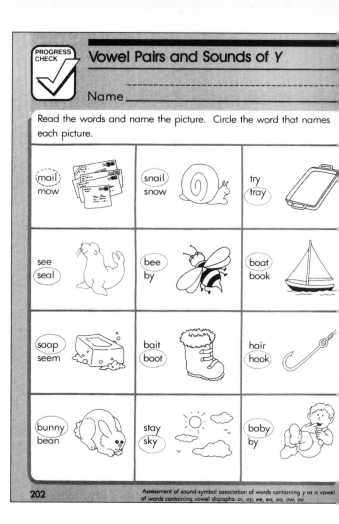

(mail) mow	(snail) snow	try (tray)
see (seal)	(bee) by	boat book
(soap) seem	bait (boot)	hair (hook)
(bunny) bean	stay (sky)	(baby) by

202

Assessment of sound-symbol association of words containing y as a vowel of words containing vowel digraphs: ai, ay, ee, ea, oo, ow, oa

---

Consonant Pairs: SH and CH

Name

The sound at the beginning of **shoe** is spelled by the letters **sh.** The sound at the beginning of **chair** is spelled by the letters **ch.**

shoe **ch**air

Name the pictures. In each row, circle the picture or pictures that begin with the same sound as the first picture.

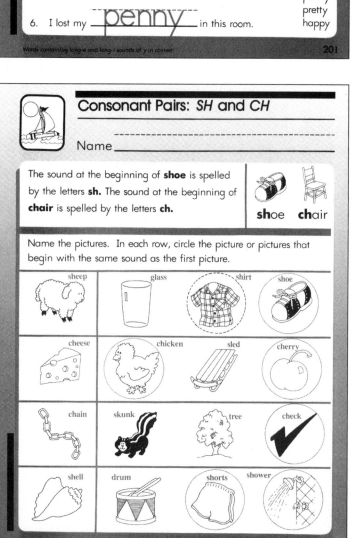

sheep	glass	shirt	shoe
cheese	chicken	sled	cherry
chain	skunk	tree	check ✔
shell	drum	shorts	shower

Auditory discrimination of initial consonant digraphs: sh, ch

203

Consonant Pairs: SH and CH

Name

Read the words below and look at the pictures. Write the word that tells about each picture.

ship	shave	chain
sheep	chop	chin
cheek	shell	shed

shoe **ch**air

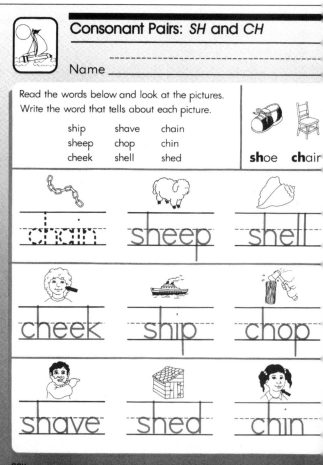

chain   sheep   shell

cheek   ship   chop

shave   shed   chin

204

Symbol-sound association of initial consonant digraph words: sh, ch

Consonant Pairs: SH and CH

Name _____

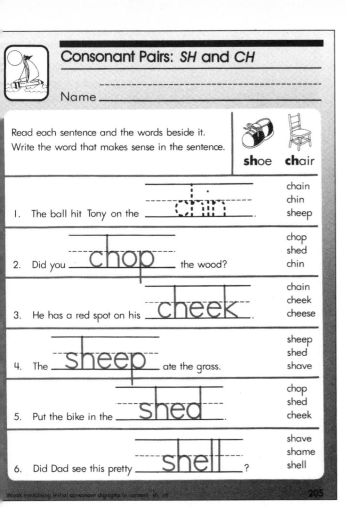

Read each sentence and the words beside it.
Write the word that makes sense in the sentence.

shoe   **ch**air

1. The ball hit Tony on the ___chin___.	chain chin sheep
2. Did you ___chop___ the wood?	chop shed chin
3. He has a red spot on his ___cheek___.	chain cheek cheese
4. The ___sheep___ ate the grass.	sheep shed shave
5. Put the bike in the ___shed___.	chop shed cheek
6. Did Dad see this pretty ___shell___?	shave shame shell

Words containing initial consonant digraphs in context: sh, ch   205

Consonant Pairs: TH and WH

Name _____

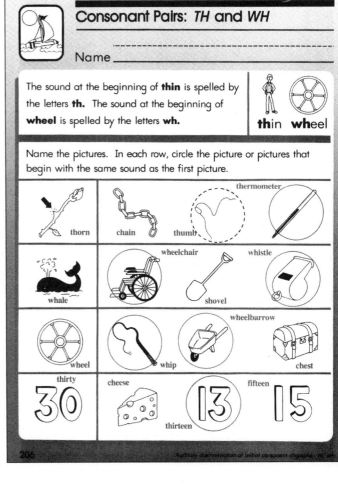

The sound at the beginning of **thin** is spelled by the letters **th.** The sound at the beginning of **wheel** is spelled by the letters **wh.**

thin   **wh**eel

Name the pictures. In each row, circle the picture or pictures that begin with the same sound as the first picture.

thorn	chain	thumb	thermometer
whale	wheelchair	shovel	whistle
wheel	whip	wheelbarrow	chest
thirty 30	cheese thirteen	13	15 fifteen

206   Auditory discrimination of initial consonant digraphs: th, wh

---

Consonant Pairs: TH and WH

Name _____

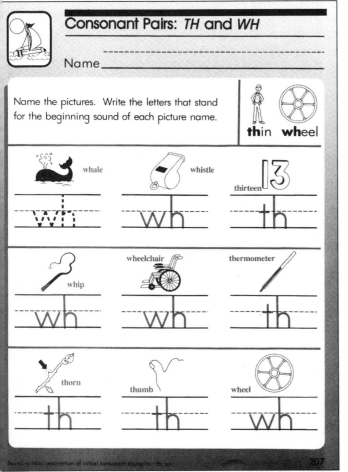

Name the pictures. Write the letters that stand for the beginning sound of each picture name.

thin   **wh**eel

whale ___wh___	whistle ___wh___	thirteen 13 ___th___
whip ___wh___	wheelchair ___wh___	thermometer ___th___
thorn ___th___	thumb ___th___	wheel ___wh___

Sound-symbol association of initial consonant digraphs: th, wh   207

Consonant Pairs: TH and WH

Name _____

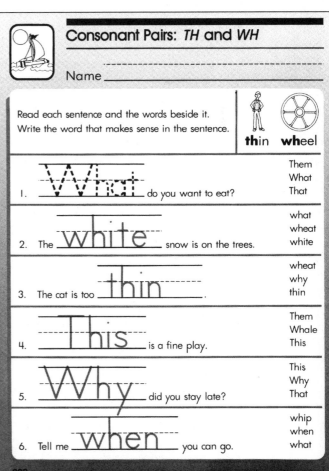

Read each sentence and the words beside it.
Write the word that makes sense in the sentence.

thin   **wh**eel

1. ___What___ do you want to eat?	Them What That
2. The ___white___ snow is on the trees.	what wheat white
3. The cat is too ___thin___.	wheat why thin
4. ___This___ is a fine play.	Them Whale This
5. ___Why___ did you stay late?	This Why That
6. Tell me ___when___ you can go.	whip when what

208   Words containing initial consonant digraphs in context: th, wh

291

Consonant Pairs: Final SH, CH, and TH

Name _____

The sound at the end of **wish** is spelled by the letters **sh**.	wi**sh**
The sound at the end of **each** is spelled by the letters **ch**.	ea**ch**
The sound at the end of **with** is spelled by the letters **th**.	wi**th**

Name the pictures. In each row, circle the picture or pictures that end with the same sound as the first picture.

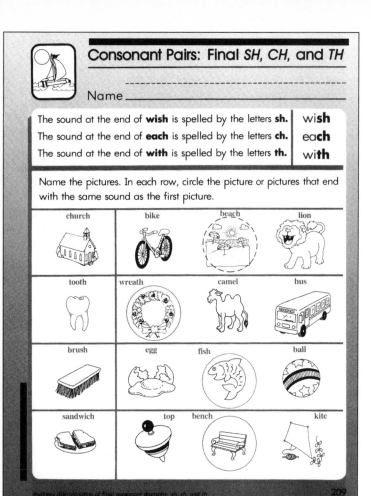

Consonant Pairs: Final SH, CH, and TH

Name _____

| Name the pictures. Write the letters that stand for the end sound of each picture name. | wi**sh** ea**ch** wi**th** |

Consonant Pairs: Final SH, CH, and TH

Name _____

| Read each sentence and the words beside it. Write the word that makes sense in the sentence. | wi**sh** ea**ch** wi**th** |

1. Did Pablo brush his ___teeth___ ?
   dish / math / teeth

2. I will ___wash___ my face.
   bush / trash / wash

3. We swim at the ___beach___.
   peach / beach / reach

4. Eva ate a ___sandwich___.
   sandwich / leash / inch

5. I gave the dog a ___bath___.
   math / path / bath

6. I broke the blue ___dish___.
   fish / wish / dish

Consonant Pairs: NG

Name _____

| The sound at the end of **ring** is spelled by the letters **ng**. | ri**ng** |

Name the pictures. Circle each picture whose name ends with **ng**.

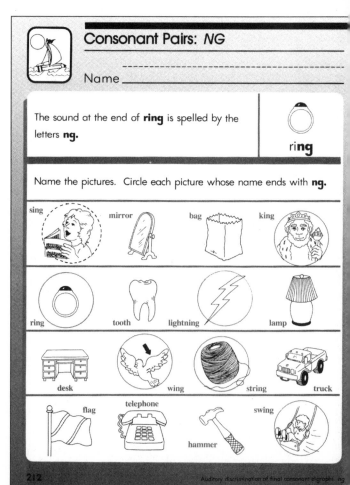

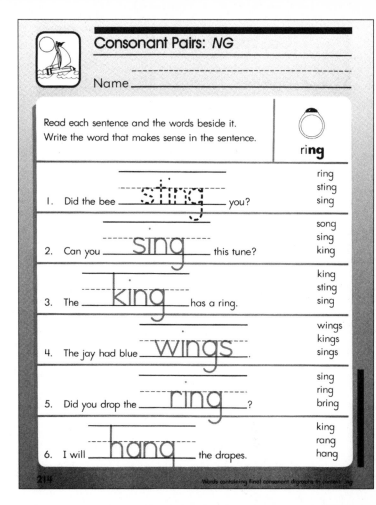

Consonant Pairs: NG

Name _____

ri**ng**

Read the words and look at the pictures. Circle the word that tells about each picture.

(swing) / sing	wing / (sing)	bang / (hang)
sting / (king)	sting / (swing)	(sing) / bring
(song) / ring	wing / (sting)	(ring) / king

Symbol-sound association of words containing final consonant digraphs: ng
213

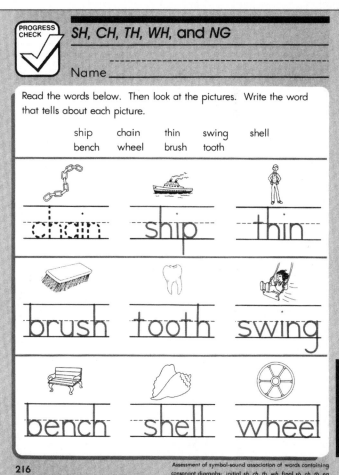

Consonant Pairs: NG

Name _____

ri**ng**

Read each sentence and the words beside it. Write the word that makes sense in the sentence.

1. Did the bee _____sting_____ you?   ring / sting / sing
2. Can you _____sing_____ this tune?   song / sing / king
3. The _____king_____ has a ring.   king / sting / sing
4. The jay had blue _____wings_____.   wings / kings / sings
5. Did you drop the _____ring_____?   sing / ring / bring
6. I will _____hang_____ the drapes.   king / rang / hang

214
Words containing final consonant digraphs in context: ng

REVIEW

SH, CH, TH, WH, and NG

Name _____

Read the words and look at the pictures. Circle the word that tells about each picture.

(wing) / sing / bring / ring	(chain) / when / then / shape	chin / (thin) / whip / ship
math / (bath) / with / path	(fish) / dish / wash / push	(whale) / shave / cheese / these
inch / each / (bench) / beach	sheep / cheap / wheat / that	ring / wing / sing / (swing)

Review of symbol-sound association of words containing consonant digraphs: initial sh, ch, th, wh, final ch, sh, th, ng
215

PROGRESS CHECK ✓

SH, CH, TH, WH, and NG

Name _____

Read the words below. Then look at the pictures. Write the word that tells about each picture.

ship   chain   thin   swing   shell
bench   wheel   brush   tooth

chain	ship	thin
brush	tooth	swing
bench	shell	wheel

216
Assessment of symbol-sound association of words containing consonant digraphs: initial sh, ch, th, wh, final sh, ch, th, ng

293

Endings: -ED and -ING

Name _____

play
play**ed**
play**ing**

Read the words below. Add **-ed** and **-ing** to each word to form new words. Write the new words in the blanks.

		Add **-ed**	Add **-ing**
1.	wait	waited	waiting
2.	look	looked	looking
3.	toss	tossed	tossing
4.	want	wanted	wanting
5.	work	worked	working
6.	jump	jumped	jumping

Adding -ed and -ing to verbs   217

Base Words and Endings: -ED and -ING

Name _____

A word to which an ending can be added is called a base word. The base word of **played** is **play.** The base word of **playing** is **play.**

play
play**ed**
play**ing**

Read each word below and write its base word.

1.	needed	need	7.	filled	fill
2.	singing	sing	8.	staying	stay
3.	passing	pass	9.	jumped	jump
4.	cleaned	clean	10.	spilling	spill
5.	loaded	load	11.	floating	float
6.	glowing	glow	12.	raining	rain

218   Identifying base words

Endings: -ED and -ING

Name _____

Read each sentence and the words beside it. Write the word that makes sense in each sentence.

1.	We _worked_ at the shop.	worked	working
2.	Tam _passed_ the shop.	passed	passing
3.	Is Grace _looking_ for a hat?	looked	looking
4.	Tony _waited_ for his mom.	waited	waiting
5.	Bob is _tossing_ the ball.	tossed	tossing
6.	Rosa is _helping_ Kim.	helped	helping
7.	Max _wanted_ to go home.	wanted	wanting

Adding endings in context: -ed, -ing   219

-ED and -ING

Name _____

Read each sentence and the word beside it. Add **-ed** or **-ing** to the word so it makes sense in the sentence. Write the word in the blank.

1.	Dan _called_ to his mom.	call
2.	The boat is _floating_ in the lake.	float
3.	Ramona is _telling_ us to go.	tell
4.	Dad _cleaned_ the room well.	clean
5.	The class will be _showing_ slides.	show
6.	We _worked_ at the shop.	work

220   Review of using context clues to add -ed and -ing to verbs

294

-ED and -ING

Name _____

Read each sentence and the endings beside it. Add one of the endings to the word shown below the blank. Write the word in the blank to complete the sentence.

1. Pat __waited__ ten days for the books.   -ed / -ing
   (wait)

2. Kim is __looking__ for the boots.   -ed / -ing
   (look)

3. The frog __jumped__ onto the log.   -ed / -ing
   (jump)

4. Jimmy will be __cleaning__ his room.   -ed / -ing
   (clean)

5. The puppy __wanted__ to eat.   -ed / -ing
   (want)

6. Will you be __staying__ late?   -ed / -ing
   (stay)

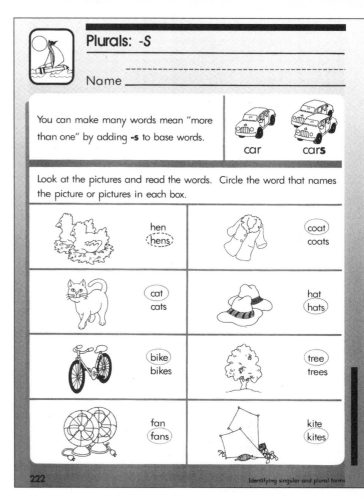

Plurals: -S

Name _____

You can make many words mean "more than one" by adding **-s** to base words.

car   car**s**

Look at the pictures and read the words. Circle the word that names the picture or pictures in each box.

hen, (hens)		(coat), coats	
(cat), cats		hat, (hats)	
(bike), bikes		(tree), trees	
fan, (fans)		kite, (kites)	

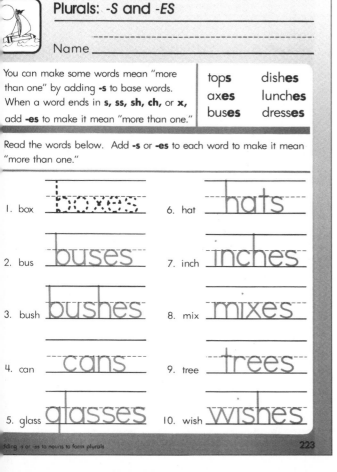

Plurals: -S and -ES

Name _____

You can make some words mean "more than one" by adding **-s** to base words. When a word ends in **s, ss, sh, ch,** or **x,** add **-es** to make it mean "more than one."

top**s**   dish**es**
ax**es**   lunch**es**
bus**es**   dress**es**

Read the words below. Add **-s** or **-es** to each word to make it mean "more than one."

1. box __boxes__   6. hat __hats__

2. bus __buses__   7. inch __inches__

3. bush __bushes__   8. mix __mixes__

4. can __cans__   9. tree __trees__

5. glass __glasses__   10. wish __wishes__

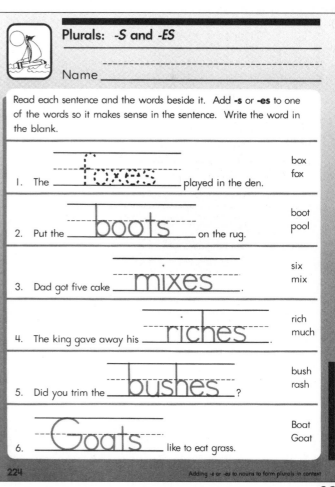

Plurals: -S and -ES

Name _____

Read each sentence and the words beside it. Add **-s** or **-es** to one of the words so it makes sense in the sentence. Write the word in the blank.

1. The __foxes__ played in the den.   box / fox

2. Put the __boots__ on the rug.   boot / pool

3. Dad got five cake __mixes__.   six / mix

4. The king gave away his __riches__.   rich / much

5. Did you trim the __bushes__?   bush / rash

6. __Goats__ like to eat grass.   Boat / Goat

Plurals: -S and -ES

Name _____

Read each sentence and the words beside it. Add **-s** or **-es** to one of the words so it makes sense in the sentence. Write the word in the blank.

1. The oak __trees__ had to be cut. — pen / tree

2. The __foxes__ ran by the lake. — fox / box

3. Jimmy made the __lunches__. — lunch / much

4. Put five __cans__ into this bag. — can / wish

5. Mike fell into the rose __bushes__. — frame / bush

6. Did you use __eggs__ in the cake mix? — hat / egg

Adding -s or -es to nouns to form plurals in context   225

REVIEW ## Plurals

Name _____

Read the words below. Add **-s** or **-es** to each word to make it mean "more than one."

1. hen __hens__   7. wish __wishes__

2. mix __mixes__   8. bus __buses__

3. lunch __lunches__   9. song __songs__

4. class __classes__   10. bird __birds__

5. coat __coats__   11. glass __glasses__

6. dish __dishes__   12. rich __riches__

226   Review of adding -s or -es to form plur

PROGRESS CHECK ✓ ## Plurals

Name _____

Read each sentence and the endings beside it. Add one of the endings to the word shown below the blank. Write the word in the blank to complete the sentence.

1. Put the __boxes__ in the den. (box) — -s / -es

2. Gail made five __wishes__. (wish) — -s / -es

3. Will you make the __beds__? (bed) — -s / -es

4. All of the __buses__ will stop here. (bus) — -s / -es

5. Take the __pans__ off the stove. (pan) — -s / -es

6. All of the __classes__ will go to the zoo. (class) — -s / -es

Assessment of adding -s or -es to form plurals in context   227

Contractions

Name _____

A contraction is a short way to write two words. It is written by putting two words together and leaving out a letter or letters. An apostrophe (') takes the place of the letter or letters that are left out.

did + not = **didn't**
I + am = **I'm**

Read the list of words below. Then read the word pairs that follow. Write a contraction from the list for each word pair.

| aren't | I'm | isn't | haven't |
| doesn't | hasn't | wasn't | didn't |

1. have not __haven't__   5. are not __aren't__

2. was not __wasn't__   6. is not __isn't__

3. I am __I'm__   7. did not __didn't__

4. does not __doesn't__   8. has not __hasn't__

228   Forming contractions using not, a

296

Contractions

Name _____

Read each contraction below. Then write the two words for which each contraction stands.

I + will = **I'll**
it + is = **it's**

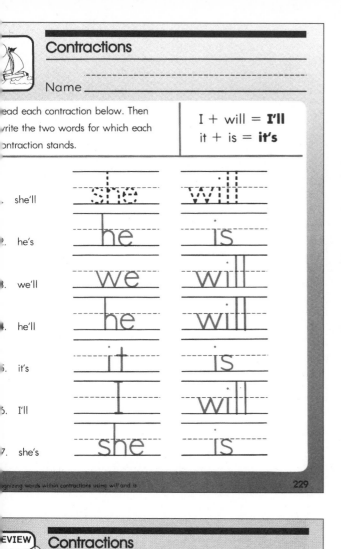

1. she'll — she will
2. he's — he is
3. we'll — we will
4. he'll — he will
5. it's — it is
6. I'll — I will
7. she's — she is

Contractions

Name _____

Read each sentence below. Write the contraction for the words shown below the blank in each sentence.

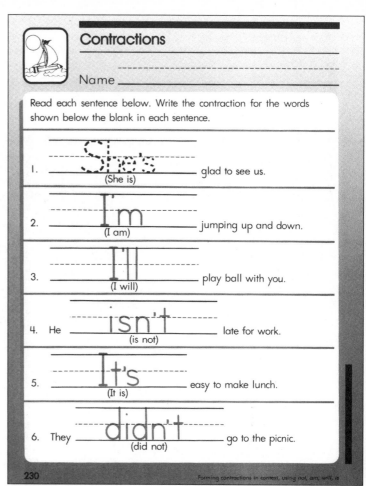

1. __She's__ glad to see us.
   (She is)
2. __I'm__ jumping up and down.
   (I am)
3. __I'll__ play ball with you.
   (I will)
4. He __isn't__ late for work.
   (is not)
5. __It's__ easy to make lunch.
   (It is)
6. They __didn't__ go to the picnic.
   (did not)

REVIEW

Contractions

Name _____

Read each sentence below. Write the contraction for the words shown below the blank in each sentence.

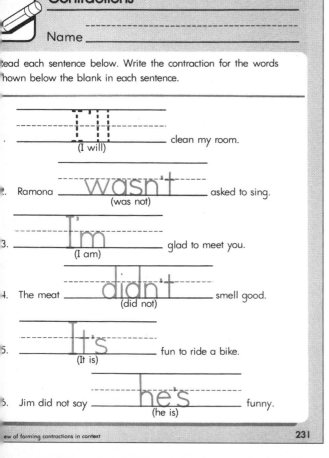

1. __I'll__ clean my room.
   (I will)
2. Ramona __wasn't__ asked to sing.
   (was not)
3. __I'm__ glad to meet you.
   (I am)
4. The meat __didn't__ smell good.
   (did not)
5. __It's__ fun to ride a bike.
   (It is)
6. Jim did not say __he's__ funny.
   (he is)

PROGRESS CHECK ✓

Contractions

Name _____

Read each pair of words below. Write the contraction for each word pair.

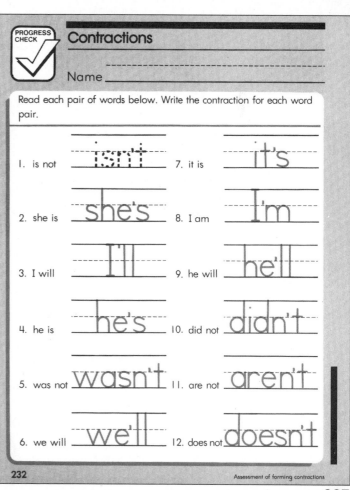

1. is not — isn't
2. she is — she's
3. I will — I'll
4. he is — he's
5. was not — wasn't
6. we will — we'll
7. it is — it's
8. I am — I'm
9. he will — he'll
10. did not — didn't
11. are not — aren't
12. does not — doesn't

ABC Order

Name_____

Each letter has its own place in the alphabet.

a b c d e f g h i j k l m
n o p q r s t u v w x y z

Look at the letters in each box. In the blank, write the missing letter. The letters in each box should be in ABC order.

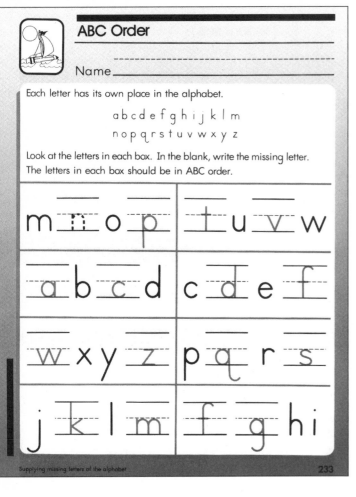

m n o p	t u v w
a b c d	c d e f
w x y z	p q r s
j k l m	f g h i

ABC Order

Name_____

a b c d e f g h i j k l m
n o p q r s t u v w x y z

Look at the letters in each box. Write the letters in ABC order.

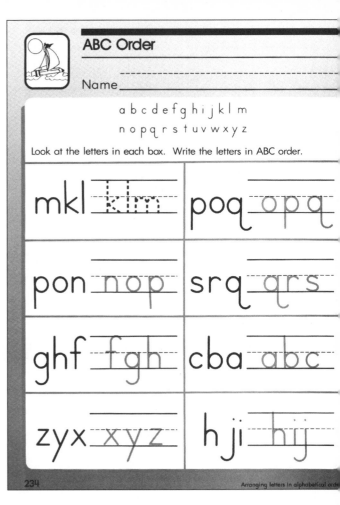

mkl klm	poq opq
pon nop	srq qrs
ghf fgh	cba abc
zyx xyz	hji hij

ABC Order

Name_____

a b c d e f g h i j k l m
n o p q r s t u v w x y z

Look at the letters in each box. Write the letters in ABC order. The letters you write should form a word.

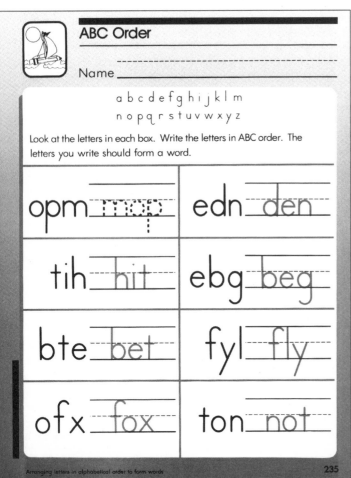

opm mop	edn den
tih hit	ebg beg
bte bet	fyl fly
ofx fox	ton not

REVIEW   ABC Order

Parent Involvement Master 4, Page 7—

Name_____

Write the missing letters to complete the alphabet.

a	b	c	d	e
f	g	h	i	j
k	l	m	n	o
p	q	r	s	t
u	v	w	x	y z

ABC Order

Name _____

Look at the letters in each box. Write the letters in ABC order. The letters you write should form a word.

onw **now**	obx **box**
tif **fit**	cto **cot**
tbi **bit**	mih **him**
ogt **got**	fni **fin**

NOTES

NOTES

NOTES

NOTES